BRITISH BISCUIT TINS

Publication of this book
has been made possible by
generous contributions from
Nabisco Group Ltd,
Rowntree Mackintosh plc
and
United Biscuits (UK) Ltd

BRITISH BISCUIT TINS

M. J. Franklin

Victoria & Albert Museum

Front Cover
DOLL'S HOUSE   c.1908
Mackenzie & Mackenzie   (M.590–1983)

Frontispiece
BISCUIT TIN BASES
Somewhat surprisingly many early tins had very
decorative bases. A selection of these from most of
the major biscuit companies, issued between 1888
and 1902, shows clearly what care and attention went
into the design of an area of the tins not normally
seen.

Facing Page
1. 'HURDY GURDY'   1912
Wm. Crawford & Sons
A rare pre World War I 'toy' biscuit tin.
(M.141–1983)

Back Cover
PARROT CAGE   c.1896   John Walker Ltd.
(M.748–1983)

ISBN 0 905209 62 1
Published by the Victoria & Albert Museum 1984

Photography by Geoffrey Shakerley,
Sally Chappell (Plate 26)
Richard Davis (Plates 12, 13, and 23)

Catalogue by Elisabeth Darby

Designed and printed by
Robert Stockwell Limited, The Southwark Press,
London. Designer: Bernard Roberts.

FOR JOSEPHINE

IF THE MAN in the street today were asked to describe a biscuit tin, he would probably think of a plain round or square metal box with a bunch of flowers, a prettified landscape or a fluffy cat pictured on the lid. Yet biscuit tins were not always so ordinary and unimaginative, and they certainly do not deserve the rather debased image they have acquired in the years since World War II. As the traditional British grocery shops with their delicious smells and their distinctive atmosphere have sadly disappeared, so too have the ornate and elaborately decorated biscuit tins that would have been on display on their shelves in bygone days. Most of the tins in this book would have been there for sale at Christmas when manufacturers traditionally packed biscuits into these unusual and eye-catching tin boxes.

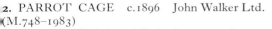

2. PARROT CAGE c.1896 John Walker Ltd. (M.748–1983)
A fine and well-designed little tin put out by a small Glasgow biscuit manufacturer.

7

3. EARLY HUNTLEY & PALMERS
TRANSFER-PRINTED TINS
Four tins made using transfers supplied by Benjamin
George George. The tin in the foreground is generally
accepted as being the first ever 'printed' British
biscuit tin.

Embossed Court c.1871 Huntley & Palmers
(M.194–1983)
Court c.1870 Huntley & Palmers (M.191–1983)
Court c.1870 Huntley & Palmers (M.193–1983)
Ben George 1868 Huntley & Palmers
(M.190–1983)

The first 'printed' British biscuit tin was produced in 1868. In that year the unforgettably named Benjamin George George, a printer trading from Hatton Garden in the City of London from 1856 to 1893, produced transfer-decorated sheets of tinplate designed by the eminent Victorian designer Owen Jones (1809–1874). Jones had been a leading designer with the Thomas de la Rue company for many years and the biscuit manufacturers Huntley & Palmers were regular clients of this noted printing firm. When in 1868 Huntley & Palmers were given permission to make it known that they were biscuit suppliers to Queen Victoria's Royal Household, Owen Jones designed a transfer incorporating the Royal Coat of Arms for Huntley & Palmers. Benjamin George George printed the design on to sheets of tinplate which were then sent to Huntley & Boorne, the metal box makers in Reading, and they made up the sheets into tin boxes for Huntley & Palmers (Plate 3).

Benjamin George George had acquired the idea of the *transfer* process after seeing the work of the Frenchman F. A. Appel at the 1862 London International Exhibition. Appel had even been awarded a medal for his 'varnished metal sheets decorated with transfers'. George, a prolific patentee in the early 1860s, realised the potential of the process and he took out several British patents. The method of decoration was in effect very similar to that used to decorate porcelain and pottery since the mid-18th century. Transfers were first laid face down on to prepared sheets of tin. When dry, the backing was soaked off leaving the design fixed to the metal. Coatings of copal varnish were then applied and the sheets finally put in an oven to harden.

4. TRANSFER-PRINTED TINS 1881–1887
Not legally entitled to use the Bryant & May's patented offset litho process, exclusive to Huntley, Boorne & Stevens until 1889, other metal box makers continued to produce transfer-decorated tins for their biscuit-making clients.
John Gilpin c.1884 Peek, Frean & Co. (M.643–1983)
Nations c.1882 Peek, Frean & Co. (M.642–1983)
'Tambour' c.1881 Peek, Frean & Co. (M.641–1983)
Marjory May c.1887 Co-Operative Wholesale Society (M.93–1983)

It had, however, been possible to print on to tin by yet another patented process before transfers came into widespread use. This was by a technique called the *direct* method. Under two separate 1864 patents issued to W. E. Gedge and P. W. and Wickham Flower (based also on an idea from the Continent) the Tin Plate Decorating Company of Neath, Glamorganshire, South Wales were direct-printing sheets of tinplate in the mid-1860s. A few tins survive 'signed' by this firm, but they are containers for products other than biscuits, the best known examples being the early tins made for the mustard manufacturers Barringer & Company of Mansfield, Nottinghamshire.

The direct method meant laying the inked stone down directly on to the sheets of tinplate. It proved only truly successful when printing one colour on to a ground of another colour. If more than one colour was used the printers had difficulty in properly lining up successive printings. There does exist a rare direct-printed Huntley & Palmers biscuit tin but no documentation has been found to indicate just who supplied the direct-decorated sheets to be made up into the biscuit tin (Plate 5).

5. FACTORY PICTURE   c.1873
Huntley & Palmers   (M.195–1983)
A rare two-colour direct-printed biscuit tin reproducing on the lid a perspective view of the firm's Reading factory.

6. EARLY HUNTLEY & PALMERS OFFSET LITHO PRINTED TINS
All these tins quote the fact on them that they have been produced using the Bryant & May assigned patented process.

Universal c.1887 Huntley & Palmers (M.215–1983)
'Sailor' 1888 Huntley & Palmers (M.224–1983)
'Sporting' 1889 Huntley & Palmers (M.225–1983)
'Coach and Horses' 1888 Huntley & Palmers (M.220–1983)
'Landscape' c.1890 Huntley & Palmers (M.229–1983)
'Orient' 1887 Huntley & Palmers (M.211–1983)

One company in the 1870s acquired the use of yet a third, and important, method of tin printing. This was Huntley, Boorne & Stevens (Stevens having become a partner of Huntley & Boorne in 1872), the metal box makers situated near their related company Huntley & Palmers in Reading, Berkshire. In 1877 they obtained the exclusive rights to an *offset lithographic* process, then owned by the London firm of match makers Bryant & May. Bryant & May had in turn acquired the patents for this process from Robert Barclay and John Doyle Fry, partners in a City of London stationery printing house.

As with the previously mentioned methods, the idea seems to have originated on the Continent. In 1875 Barclay and Fry happened to meet 'Henry Baber of Paris'. Mr Baber was in fact an Englishman who had just returned to England after having worked in France for the past four years. There he had seen the 'new' process for printing on to tin and, for a reported sum of £5, told Barclay and Fry all he had seen and learnt of the method when he met them in London.

Barclay and Fry took out two patents in 1875 for this process, known now as offset litho tin printing, which even today remains the main method for printing on to tin. Barclay and Fry seem to have had insufficient confidence or capital, or a combination of both, to set up a factory to use the process themselves, so they looked for another firm to sell their patents to. After two years the patents were assigned to Messrs Bryant & May.

The offset lithographic process had major advantages over both the previously mentioned methods. The design was first printed on to flat, glazed cardboard (soon after on to rubber-covered sheets – rotary presses were not introduced until 1903) and then offset on to the tinplate. No longer did the stone come into direct contact with the metal and this process had no difficulty in coping with many colours correctly positioned. Huntley, Boorne & Stevens were the only firm legally entitled to print tin using the Bryant & May process from 1877 until after the 1875 patent ran out in 1889. Most of the tins they produced during that period bear the mark 'B & M Pat' (Plate 6). However, there is much evidence that other British metal box makers did not wait until 1889 before they too started offset litho printing. Hudson Scott & Sons of Carlisle almost certainly did some offset work prior to 1889. In a way this is not all that surprising, in that the same Henry Baber, who had originally brought the idea from France, worked for the Carlisle firm from 1877 until his death in 1929.

As soon as the patents ran out in 1889, all the metal printing firms in Britain had machinery installed so that they too could print by the improved method and try and catch up with the lead that Huntley, Boorne & Stevens had established in the field.

7. 'WILDFLOWER' 1887 Huntley & Palmers (M.216–1983)
A rare and boldly decorated tin bearing the mark 'B & M Pat'.

Looking at tins nowadays, it is a pity that virtually all transfer-decorated tins (costly and time-consuming to make due to all the handwork involved) ceased to be produced after 1889. Of all the methods used to decorate tinplate this process produced tins of an incomparable subtle charm (Plate 8). Over the years transfers acquire an attractive and delicate *craquelure* similar to that found in old paintings. Yet there is no doubt that it was the advent of offset lithographic printed tin that made it possible to produce the ornate and inventively shaped tins that were to come.

8. 'JUBILEE' 1887 Carr & Co. (M.40–1983)
A fine transfer-printed tin brought out to celebrate H.M. Queen Victoria's Golden Jubilee. The pictures on the sides depict the royal residences: Windsor Castle, Osborne House, Holyrood Palace and Balmoral Castle.

Biscuits in Victorian times were an early example of a food that was socially acceptable to have bought in a shop. They were not strictly a luxury item but certainly the biscuits bought in a decorated tin, costing as much as a shilling more, were regarded as such. The decorated or 'enamelled' tins as they were called in the trade were aimed at the middle classes. The poor would usually only ever buy biscuits loose, often bags of broken pieces. Oddly the gentry also would have bought their biscuits loose, although whole, and they would have rarely seen a tin on the tea table, for their biscuits would have been decanted and brought from the kitchen to the table on plates.

Many of the new tins brought out at Christmas were designed to appeal to children (Plate 11). Most biscuit firms in the early 1890s started putting out small tins, called 'Juvenile' tins, which were decorated with a picture or a story with children in mind. These small tins contained few biscuits. They were clearly not made to sell large quantities of biscuits but to sell as decorated tins. They must have proved ideal 'stocking fillers'. In the case of the most charming series of little 'Juvenile' tins put out by Carr & Co. in the early 1890s, an illustrated paper label was pasted inside the lid giving Carr's name as well as the title or name of the tin (Plate 9).

9. 'JUVENILE No. 2 (SQUARE)' c.1892
Carr & Co. (M.52–1983)
A tin fron the series of little 'Juvenile' tins put out by
Carr's in the 1890s.

10. CHRISTMAS BISCUITS c.1880
Huntley & Palmers (M.205–1983)
A fine offset litho printed tin with the company's monogram appearing within the floral decoration on the sides.

Early biscuit tins had often prominently featured the company's name on the outside of the tin, though it soon became apparent that it was unacceptable to have this overt advertising in Victorian homes. By the mid-1880s the baker's name started to appear only on the base (Frontispiece) or inside the lid, although sometimes the firm's initials were still cunningly introduced into the decoration (Plate 10). In the archives of the metal box makers Barringer, Wallis & Manners are records of letters written to the firm by Lewis Carroll at the time they produced their 1892 'ALICE' tin. Carroll had given his permission but when he later saw the tin put out by the baker W & R Jacob & Co., with that firm's name on the base and inside the lid on a paper label, he wrote the metal box makers saying that they had 'vulgarised the boxes by turning them into advertisement mediums' (*sic*).

By the 1890s it is apparent that the biscuit companies were very well aware of the added source of revenue and were promoting their Christmas tins as attractive objects in their own right, many obviously intended to be kept long after the contents had been consumed. *The Grocer* magazine, the grocery trade's journal, even started producing a column each autumn in which they reviewed the season's new tins; such-and-such a firm's tins 'will surely find favour with the public this Christmas' or another firm's tins 'were not up to the usual standard of enamelled boxes we have come to expect from this company'. Rarely were the contents mentioned.

11. VICTORIAN AND EDWARDIAN TINS FEATURING CHILDREN

Not only were many biscuit tins conceived to appeal to children, but also children as a subject matter of the tins' decoration proved very popular and they interestingly record children's dress and pastimes.

'*Chums*' 1911 Wm. Crawford & Sons (M.139–1983)

'*Fireside*' c.1890 Huntley & Palmers (M.233–1983)

'*Seasons*' c.1892 Carr & Co. (M.51–1983)

Urchins c.1890 Wm. Crawford & Sons (M.134–1983)

'*Seaside*' 1890 Huntley & Palmers (M.230–1983)

'*Post Office*' 1904 Gray, Dunn & Co. (M.184–1983)

'*Juvenile No. 1*' 1895 Carr & Co. (M.56–1983)

'*See Saw*' 1905 Gray, Dunn & Co. (M.185–1983)

Our Darlings c.1913 Gray, Dunn & Co. (M.188–1983)

'*Juvenile*' c.1890 Carr & Co. (M.43–1983)

Pets c.1890 Co-Operative Wholesale Society (M.94–1983)

'*Silver*' 1904 Peek, Frean & Co. (M.667–1983)

'*See Saw*' 1906 W & R Jacob (M.462–1983)

Children 1888 Peek, Frean & Co. (M.645–1983)

16

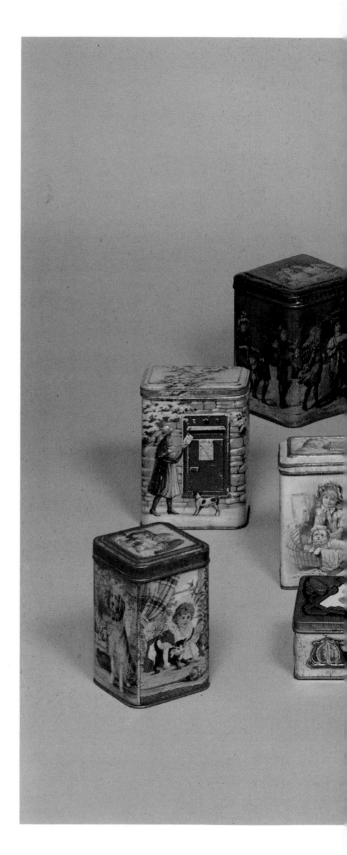

12. PEEK, FREAN & CO's 'DERBY' TIN
The company's tin is shown alongside a brochure
sent out to grocers to announce the new biscuit tin.

'Derby' 1902 Peek, Frean & Co. (M.665–1983)
Brochure 1902 Peek, Frean & Co. (E.2093–1983)

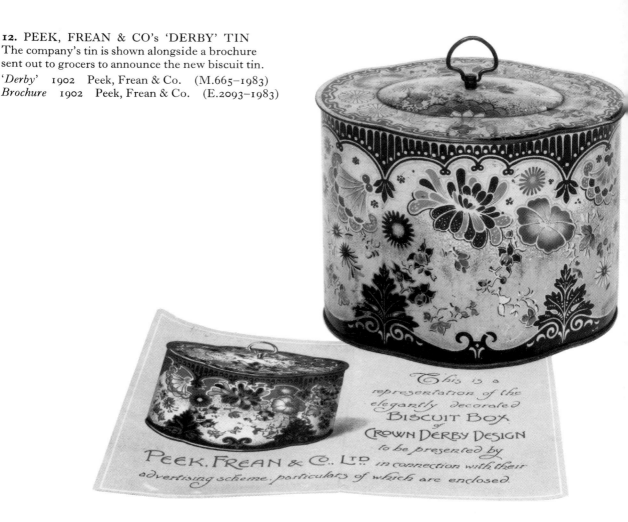

The biscuit companies annually issued handsome coloured booklets showing their biscuits and their new Christmas tins. Many times a special promotion was done for a new tin. Not only was an attractive coloured brochure put out by Peek Frean & Co. to announce their 'DERBY' tin of 1902 (Plate 12) but the firm also had a series of postcards sent out to regular customers whose names had been supplied to the bakers by grocers (Plate 13). All this material is of course invaluable in researching the date when a given tin first appeared.

13. PROMOTIONAL POSTCARDS   1907
Peek, Frean & Co.   (E.2230–1983 to E.2232–1983)
A set of three postcards sent out, at weekly intervals,
to customers whose names had been given to the
biscuit firm by the grocers. Although the 'Derby'
tin had first come out in 1902 these postcards did not
appear until 1907; a further set, showing a lady
receiving a 'Derby' tin, came out in 1908.

It was becoming increasingly important for the biscuit manufacturers to try and better one another by offering their Christmas biscuits in more and more elaborate and striking tins. On the Continent these Christmas tins were called *boites de fantasie*, a particularly apt name for the fantastic boxes being dreamt up and made by the metal box makers in Britain to contain the humble biscuit.

Little evidence has been found to indicate that the biscuit makers told the metal box makers what form the tins should take. Each early autumn the metal box makers would also send out extensively illustrated booklets showing what tins their designers had conceived during the past 12 months. From these, each biscuit company would choose which tins they wanted to use for the forthcoming Christmas season. A company could either buy exclusive rights to a tin or, for a lesser fee, buy the rights to a design for one year only. It is not unusual to see an enamelled tin of one design issued in successive years by more than one biscuit company. The metal box makers aimed their best and most eye-catching tins at the biscuit firms, for biscuit tins were always regarded in their trade as the 'top end of the market'.

14. TINS FEATURING FAMOUS PERSONS
A most unusual tin in this group is the Charnley tin
which has pictures of famous actresses on it, namely
Lily Langtry as Rosalind, Ellen Terry as Marguerite
in 'Faust' and the American Mary Anderson on the lid.
'Columbus' 1892 W & R Jacob (M.447–1983)
'African Heroes' 1892 McVitie & Price
(M.597–1983)
Burns c.1891 Gray, Dunn & Co.
(M.176–1983)
Actresses c.1891 Thomas Charnley (M.699–1983)
'Tennyson' 1894 Carr & Co. (M.55–1983)
'Shakespeare' 1892 Gray, Dunn & Co.
(M.177–1983)

Up to the 1900s tins usually featured pictures of children, flowers, birds and well-
known places as their decoration. Often,
famous persons were depicted, though
rarely anyone living; a rare and interesting
exception being a tin used by a small
Preston, Lancs. bakers on which famous
actresses of the day are shown (Plate 14).
The Royal Family were often featured.
Biscuit tins, like commemorative mugs and
other similar items, were issued by almost
all the biscuit manufacturers to celebrate
and record Royal events like Coronations
and Jubilees (Plate 15).

15. ROYAL COMMEMORATIVE TINS
1887–1911

'Diamond Jubilee' 1897 Peek, Frean & Co.
(M.658–1983)
Golden Jubilee 1887 Huntley & Palmers
(M.214–1983)
'Coronation' 1902 Carr & Co. (M.68–1983)
'Coronation—Juvenile' 1902 Carr & Co.
(M.69–1983)
'Royalty' 1901 Gray, Dunn & Co.
(M.180–1983)
Coronation 1911 Mackenzie & Mackenzie
(M.594–1983)

However, in the late 1890s tins shaped as actual objects began to be produced, all manner of baskets being almost the first to make an appearance (Plate 16). Soon after came tins as books (Plate 25), vases, and even pieces of furniture (Plate 29). A little later tins began simulating fine art objects, a further indication of another market, in addition to children, that the biscuit tins were being aimed at. The increasingly affluent and better educated middle classes could still not afford most fine art objects, but their growing pretensions were being taken into consideration by the makers and

16. TINS MADE TO SIMULATE BASKETS
The copying of baskets made of wicker, straw and rush was a popular and effective theme for biscuit tins at the turn of the century.

'*Basket*' 1897 Huntley & Palmers (M.271–1983)
'*Basket*' 1898 W & R Jacob (M.453–1983)
'*Hamper*' 1904 Huntley & Palmers (M.304–1983)
'*Creel*' 1907 Huntley & Palmers (M.322–1983)
Basket c.1898 W. Dunmore & Son (M.707–1983)
Straw Basket c.1898 A1 Biscuit Co. (M.696–1983)
'*Canteen*' 1901 Huntley & Palmers (M.291–1983)
Crescent Basket c.1898 W. Dunmore & Son (M.708–1983)
Work Basket c.1898 Palmer Bros. (M.743–1983)
Small Hamper c.1900 Palmer Bros. (M.744–1983)

the users of biscuit tins. Clearly the public were meant to buy a pair of tins in the form of vases (Plate 30) and then use them as such. Replicas of Chinese, Royal Derby and Royal Worcester porcelain were made to fuel this middle-class desire to possess *objets d'art* they knew to be in grand homes and on view in museums (Plate 17). Some of the most bizarre were the tins that had lids made as framed famous paintings. These were made by the metal box makers with a hook on the back of the lid so that the lid could be hung as a painting in one's own home (Plate 18), a precursor of to-day's popular photo reproductions.

17. TINS SIMULATING CERAMIC WARES
Generally the decoration, not always the shape, was the inspiration of the tins made to simulate ceramic items.

'Wedgwood' 1909
Macfarlanc, Lang & Co.
(M.531–1983)
'Worcester Vase' 1912
Huntley & Palmers
(M.361–1983)
'Chinese Vases' 1928
Huntley & Palmers
(M.404 & a–1983)
'Wedgwood' 1902
Macfarlane, Lang & Co.
(M.513–1983)
'Worcester Biscuit Jar' 1901
W & R Jacob
(M.456–1983)
'Derby' 1902
Peek, Frean & Co.
(M.665–1983)
'Toby Jug' 1911
Huntley & Palmers
(M.356–1983)

'Delft' 1909
Huntley & Palmers
(M.339–1983)
'Plates' 1906
Huntley & Palmers
(M.315–1983)
'Nankin' 1910
Huntley & Palmers
(M.342–1983)

18. 'LOUVRE' 1909 McVitie & Price
(M.613–1983)
The famous painting reproduced on the lid of this tin is the self portrait, with daughter, by Mme Vigée-Le Brun (1755–1842) owned by the Louvre in Paris.

23

19. TOY BISCUIT TINS OF
THE 20s AND 30s
The rarity nowadays of some of these tins is due to
the fact that all were intended as toys for children to
play with after the contents had been consumed.

'Penny in the Slot'   1923   Huntley & Palmers
(M.387–1983)
Dartboard   c.1928   W. Dunmore & Son
(M.714–1983)
'Humming Top'   1928   W & R Jacob (M.472–198_

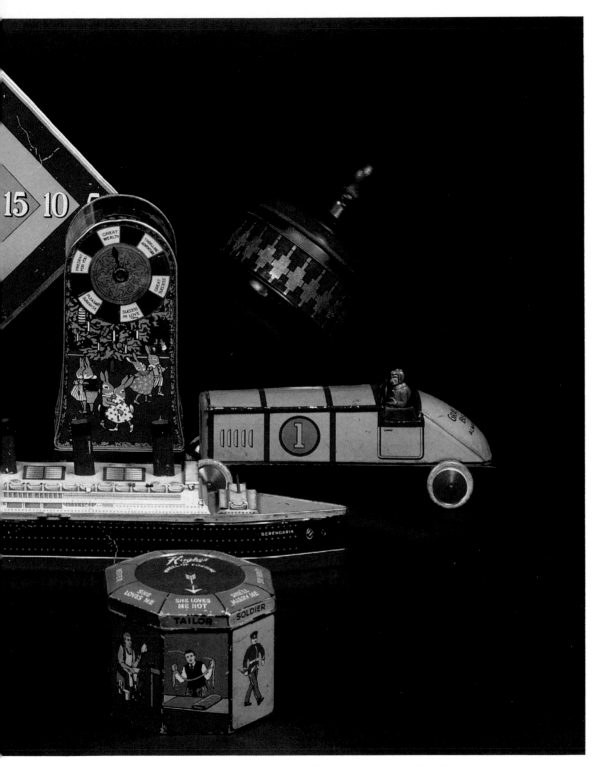

'*Caravan*' 1937 W & R Jacob (M.488–1983)
Scales c.1925 Co-Operative Wholesale Society (M.117–1983)
'*Lucky Wheel*' 1929 W & R Jacob (M.474–1983)
'*Racing Motor Car*' c.1926 Gray, Dunn & Co. (M.189–1983)

'*Menagerie*' 1933 Wm. Crawford & Sons (M.159–1983)
'*Atlantic Liner*' 1927 Wm. Crawford & Sons (M.150–1983)
'*Houseboat*' 1923 W & R Jacob (M.465–1983)
Wheel of Fortune c.1934 Hughes, Ltd (M.732–1983)

20. TINS OF THE LATE 1920s AND 1930s
'*Spanish*' 1936 Huntley & Palmers (M.431–1983)
'*Walnut Tea Caddy*' 1937 Wm. Crawford & Sons
(M.167–1983)
'*Crinoline*' 1932 Macfarlane, Lang & Co.
(M.556–1983)
'*Tea Caddy*' 1938 Macfarlane, Lang & Co.
(M.576–1983)
'*Tulip*' 1929 Peek, Frean & Co. (M.677–1983)
'*Highland*' 1936 Carr & Co. (M.89–1983)
'*Primroses*' 1930 Co-Operative Wholesale Society
(M.123–1983)
'*Daffodil*' 1934 Macfarlane, Lang & Co.
(M.561–1983)
'*Balloons*' 1930 Co-Operative Wholesale Society
(M.122–1983)
'*Como*' 1935 Co-Operative Wholesale Society
(M.131–1983)
'*Kashmir*' 1930 Peek, Frean & Co. (M.678–1983)
'*Marjorie*' 1936 W & R Jacob (M.485–1983)

The biscuit trade seriously considered whether or not to resume selling their biscuits in decorated tins after the Great War. The companies who did decide to do so did not start to order in any great quantities until after 1922, some four years after the Government lifted their restrictions on the use of metal for 'fancy' tins brought in at the outset of the war. The uncertain post-war times found the manufacturers unsure of the public taste. The new prevalent artistic style, Art Deco, was rarely used as decoration or shaping; certainly it never had as great an influence on the decoration of biscuit tins as had Art Nouveau in the years around 1900. The metal box makers' stock catalogues during this period certainly show that they were aware of the currently fashionable styles, proving that it was their cautious biscuit-making customers who decided only to order tins of plain shapes and rather ordinary decoration. The cost of the boxes had of course risen dramatically after the war and maybe it was for this reason, more than any other, that the British biscuit manufacturers reverted to plain-shaped tins with 'pretty' pictures on the lids.

For any truly fanciful, unusual and ingenious biscuit tins during this time, one again has to thank the influence of children. The biscuit manufacturers were certain (rightly, as it happened) that they could still count on this aspect of their market at Christmastime. Many of these tins aimed at children became even more elaborate and contrived. Tins in the shape of trains (Plate 21), ships, trucks and cars (even with battery-operated headlamps), dartboards and dice games, were marketed with great success (Plate 19).

Before the war, Gray, Dunn & Co. had put out a tin in the shape of a concertina; after the war, W & R Jacob went one better and put out a concertina tin that actually played (albeit only two notes). However, the biscuit tins intended for their adult customers were a different matter, for they fell back on endless depictions of bunches of flowers, well-known paintings or country scenes on their lids. If, for adults, there was any marked new feature, it was the advent of biscuit tins entitled 'TEA CADDIES'. How odd that the manufacturers of one product should so consciously steer their empty containers into use for another food product!

21. 'ENGINE' 1937 Macfarlane, Lang & Co. (M.574–1983)
A fine toy biscuit tin in the shape of the L.N.E.R. locomotive 'Silver Link', the engine that was used to draw the Silver Jubilee train between London and Newcastle.

22. TINS BY KNOWN DESIGNERS
The tins illustrated are among the very few directly
attributable to known designers, namely Mabel Lucie
Attwell (1879–1946) and Paul Greville Hudson
(1876–1960).
'*Fairy Tree*' 1935 Wm. Crawford & Sons
(M.162–1983)
'*Bicky House*' 1933 Wm. Crawford & Sons
(M.158–1983)
'*Fairy House*' 1934 Wm. Crawford & Sons
(M.161–1983)
'*Japanese*' c.1902 Gray, Dunn & Co.
(M.181–1983)
'*Ivory Casket*' 1910 Wm. Crawford & Sons
(M.137–1983)

In the 1930s there were interesting, sadly
short-lived, attempts to have well-known
British artists design tins for some of the
biscuit companies. (Very few of the names
of the designers of the Victorian and
Edwardian tins were ever recorded.) Three
highly individual tins were designed for
William Crawford & Sons by Mabel Lucie
Attwell (1879–1964) between 1933 and
1935 (Plate 22). The same firm had com-
missioned the noted Scots painter Robert
Burns (1869–1941) to design many fine
brochures and labels for them in the late
1920s; but sadly no actual biscuit tins.

Less well known were the biscuit tins
designed as a result of the Curwen Press
and Charles Barker Ltd. together com-
missioning a series of tins from young
artists such as Edward Bawden (born 1903)
for the Tunbridge Wells biscuit makers
Romary & Co. These tins were afforded
serious artistic consideration when they
came out and were even written about by
Paul Nash, and in the March 1934 issue of
Design for Today Bawden's tin was reviewed by Noel Carrington (Plate 23).

23. A BISCUIT TIN BY EDWARD BAWDEN
1934   Romary & Co.   (M.746–1983)
Edward Bawden based the lid decoration on an old print showing the young Princess Victoria on a visit to Tunbridge Wells, Kent, in 1822.

The British metal box makers in the depressed 1930s were grateful that the biscuit trade continued ordering any fancy tins at all. It was not until the end of the 1930s that the industry was on the road to full recovery. Then World War II erupted. Just when tins were starting to do what the earlier Victorian and Edwardian tins had done so well – mirror and record contemporary fashions, artistic styles and the nation's pleasures – the Government had again to call a halt to all non-essential use of metal as they had done in 1914. Factories once more had to turn their tin into containers for rations, medical supplies and ammunition.

24. ROYAL COMMEMORATIVE TINS
1935–1937
Coronation Coach   1936
W & R Jacob   (M.484–1983)
Silver Jubilee   1935
Bee Bee Biscuits Ltd.
(M.698–1983)
Silver Jubilee   1935
McVitie & Price   (M.626–1983)
Silver Jubilee   1935
Andrew G. Kidd
(M.734–1983)
Silver Jubilee   1935
Co-Operative Wholesale Society
(M.132–1983)
Coronation Edward VIII   1937
Peek, Frean & Co.   (M.691–1983)
'Coronation'   1937
Huntley & Palmers
(M.433–1983)
Coronation   1937
Wm. Crawford & Sons
(M.169–1983)

25. 'LITERATURE' 1901 Huntley & Palmers
(M.290–1983)
Biscuit tins in the shape of books were an especially
popular theme for tins made by Huntley, Boorne &
Stevens and put out by Huntley & Palmers.
'*Literature*' was the first in a series of tins in the shape
of eight leather-bound books held together by a strap.

FOR MORE THAN 60 YEARS the
metal box makers of Great Britain
had given admirable service.
Before 1914 there had been numerous companies, both large and
small, who had made the charming and appealing tins, many of
which were bought and used by
the biscuit trade. After the Great
War only a few small independent
companies survived. The pion-
eers, those with a lasting and in-
fluential position in the history of
British biscuit tins, are briefly
summarised on the
following pages.

Firstly, one must mention Huntley, Boorne & Stevens of Reading, for it was this company that had made the first ever British 'printed' biscuit tin in 1868. Close by, and related to, the biscuit manufacturers Huntley & Palmers, these metal box makers had had many advantages, the most important of which was the acquisition of sole rights to the offset lithographic process in 1877. Until 1889 they were without doubt the market leaders. However, after that date, when all the other metal box making firms in Great Britain were able to produce boxes using the revolutionary process, they were not always able to hold on to their lead. In 1918 Huntley, Boorne & Stevens came under the direct ownership of Huntley & Palmers, for whom of course they had made and continued to make many, although not all, of the biscuit company's tins. The firm had an especially hard time during the depressed 1930s but they remained the metal box making division of Huntley & Palmers and did not

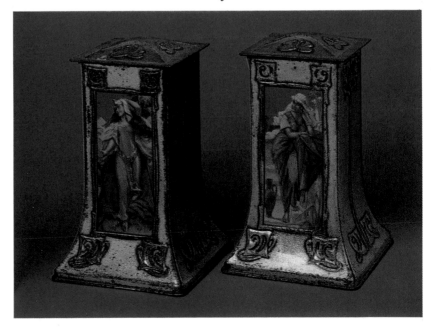

26. 'CELTIC VASES' 1905
Carr & Co. (M.76 & a–1983)
A handsome pair of vases made by
Hudson, Scott & Co. clearly inspired
by the then fashionable 'Tudric'
pewterware made for Liberty & Co.

27. LIGHTHOUSE c.1894 W. Dunmore & Son
(M.705-1983)
An early Barclay & Fry tin made with a slot for
after-use as a money-box.

merge with any of the other metal box makers in Great Britain. In 1982 they came under the ownership, as part of the sale of Huntley & Palmers, of the American company Nabisco.

A similar situation existed in Carlisle, in that there was in the same town a metal box maker, Hudson Scott & Sons, and a biscuit manufacturer, Carr & Co. Hudson Scott had been printers there from the late 1700s. They became transfer tinplate printers in 1876 and were particularly fine designers of transfer-decorated sheets, many of which they had supplied to Carr & Co. Carr's themselves made these sheets up into their own boxes until the late 1880s when Hudson Scott became metal box makers as well as tinplate printers. Throughout the years Carr & Co. were loyal to the local metal box makers and the great majority of Carr's tins were made in Carlisle.

Messrs Barclay & Fry, the company who had parted with the important offset litho process in 1877, remained 'Stationers and Printers, Account-book Makers, Cheque and Bank Note Printers, Designers and Engravers, Chromo-Lithographers, and Law Stationers' until some time in the early 1890s, when they also set up a factory in south London to print tin and make metal boxes. One of the very first must have been the 'signed' LIGHTHOUSE tin they made for a South Wigston biscuit manufacturer (Plate 27).

Happily, of a fourth firm, Barringer, Wallis & Manners, much is known of their history due largely to interesting notes on the early history of the firm written in the late 1920s by Isaac Henry Wallis. In 1879

28. 'LADIES RECREATIONS' c.1893
Mackenzie & Mackenzie (M.586–1983)
A charmingly evocative Barringer, Wallis & Manners
tin showing fashionably dressed ladies partaking in
the few sports then socially acceptable for them to
play in public.

Wallis had become a partner of the firm, which was based in Mansfield. The company had been founded in 1830 as Barringer & Company, mustard makers. In the late 1860s Robert Barringer conceived the idea of having his large tins of dry mustard packed into decorated tin boxes, from which grocers would sell small quantities as required by customers. For these tins Barringer ordered direct-printed sheets from the Tin Plate Decorating Company in South Wales, and then had two men in his Mansfield factory make them up into boxes. In 1889 the firm not only changed its name to Barringer, Wallis & Manners, but it also installed plant to print its own tinplate and enlarged its box making departments. Documents still survive in the Barringer, Wallis & Manners archives proving that they made the 'LADIES RECREATIONS' tin (Plate 28). It is also recorded that Armitage & Ibbotson of Bradford supplied the 'drawing on stone', in other words the litho stones, for the tin. Sadly the name of the artist was not similarly recorded.

The Mansfield firm went on to become one of the most successful of all British metal box makers; their products were especially popular with the biscuit manufacturers. They continue to this day, under the giant umbrella of the Metal Box Company, who also took over Hudson, Scott & Sons, Barclay & Fry and numerous other smaller independent tin box makers in the years between the two World Wars.

29. TINS SIMULATING WOODEN OBJECTS
Biscuit tins simulating wood boxes, furniture and
the like were a popular theme from Victorian times
right up into the 1930s.

'*Russian Jugs*' 1911 Wm. Crawford & Sons
(M.138 & a–1983)
'*Delia*' 1910 McVitie & Price (M.615–1983)
'*Cabinet*' 1911 Huntley & Palmers (M.351–1983)
'*Milk Can*' c.1900 S. Henderson & Sons
(M.719–1983)
'*Caucasian*' 1911 Huntley & Palmers
(M.353–1983)
'*Chippendale*' 1904 Macfarlane, Lang & Co.
(M.519–1983)
'*Roll Top Desk*' c.1901 McVitie & Price
(M.606–1983)
'*Tea Caddy*' 1938 W & R Jacob (M.489–1983)
'*Antique Tea Caddy*' 1928 Wm. Crawford & Sons
(M.152–1983)
'*Violin Case*' 1903 Macfarlane, Lang & Co.
(M.514–1983)
'*Jewel Casket*' 1898 W & R Jacob (M.454–1983)
'*Pokerwork*' 1900 Macfarlane, Lang & Co.
(M.503–1983)
'*Oak*' 1892 Huntley & Palmers (M.242–1983)
'*Maplewood Casket*' 1926 Huntley & Palmers
(M.394–1983)
Oak Barrel c.1899 W. Dunmore & Son
(M.709–1983)

One should, of course, more correctly refer
to a particular tin by the maker's name and
not just by the name of the biscuit company
that bought and used the tin. However,
this is not always possible, for not all
makers 'signed' their tins. Also, much
documentation has been lost or destroyed
over the years, making the correct attribu-
tion to the tins' actual makers difficult.
Yet it is to the metal box makers of Great
Britain, who conceived and made these
charming bygones, that the credit is due.

To end, I quote from the February 14th 1900 issue of the Victorian periodical called *Commerce*. In writing about a particular metal box maker they effectively penned a lasting tribute to the industry as a whole:

'In years to come they will have deserved the distinction of having turned the course of high art into the most utilitarian channels within reach of rich and poor.'

30. 'VASES' 1900   Peek, Frean & Co.
(M.664 & a–1983)
By placing the lid, upside down, on the bottom of the empty tin, these biscuit tins converted into flower vases.

32. TINS WITH THEIR ORIGINAL
CARDBOARD BOXES
In the 1920s and 1930s, selected, usually toy and
novelty, tins came boxed in cardboard boxes. Most
of these boxes had an illustration plus a description
of the tin enclosed.

'*Globe*'   1938   Wm. Crawford & Sons
(M.170–1983)
'*Coronation Coach*'   1936   W & R Jacob
(M.484–1983)
'*Water-mill*'   1938   Macfarlane, Lang & Co.
(M.578–1983)
'*Dice Casket*'   1929   Carr & Co.   (M.86–1983)
'*Engine*'   1937   Macfarlane, Lang & Co.
(M.574–1983)
'*Wood and Ivory Box*'   1931   Huntley & Palmers
(M.413–1983)

31. TINS IN THE SHAPE OF BUILDINGS
'*Windmill*'   1924   Huntley & Palmers
(M.388–1983)
Cheese Sandwich Inn   c.1934   Meredith & Drew
(M.741–1983)
Lighthouse   c.1894   W. Dunmore & Son
(M.705–1983)
'*Signal Box*'   1914   Co-Operative Wholesale
Society   (M.109–1983)
Greenhouse   c.1905   Far Famed Cake Co.
(M.716–1983)
'*Farmhouse*'   1931   Huntley & Palmers
(M.411–1983)

BIBLIOGRAPHY

ADAM, James S. *A Fine Fell Baker*
Hutchinson Benham   London 1974

CORLEY, T. A. B.   *Quaker Enterprise in
Biscuits
Huntley & Palmers of Reading 1822–1972*
Hutchinson   London 1972

DAVIS, Alec *Package and Print*
Faber & Faber   London 1967

FRANKLIN, M. J.   *British Biscuit Tins
1868–1939*
New Cavendish Books   London 1970

MOSES, Hannah   'A Short History of the
Hudson Scott Branch of the Metal Box
Company'   Unpublished manuscript   1962

READER, W. J.   *Metal Box, a History*
Heinemann   London 1976

WALLIS, Isaac H.   'Notes on the History
of Tin Box Making in Mansfield'
Unpublished manuscript   c. 1929

PERIODICALS
The Grocer   (1861 to the present day)
Commerce   (1893–1904)

CATALOGUE

In this catalogue biscuit tins issued by the major British biscuit manufacturers precede those of smaller companies. The companies are arranged alphabetically within these two groups and the tins are listed in date order within each company.

The name or title of the biscuit tin is given in quotation marks when it has been verified from catalogues or other documentary evidence. Names without quotation marks are those used by the tin box manufacturers, or, where no documentation was available, the title is based on the decoration of the tin itself.

All tins are rectangular, square or circular unless stated otherwise; all dimensions are maximum unless stated otherwise.

Not listed in this catalogue, but also part of the M. J. Franklin gift to the museum, are the following: Over one hundred miniature and free sample tins and over forty novelty and metal advertising items, issued by the biscuit companies, in the Department of Metalwork (M.752–1983 to M.906–1983; M.930–1983 and M.931–1983). Over eight hundred items—company catalogues, brochures, posters, and other paper ephemera —are to be found in the Department of Prints and Drawings (E.1466–1983 to E.2315–1983). Further items are in Ceramics Department (C.264–1983 to C.284–1983), Textile and Dress Department (T.274–1983) and Sculpture Department (A.47–1983 to A.56–1983).

ELISABETH DARBY

33. POCKET CALENDARS 1883–1912
(E.1926–1983 to E.1930–1983, E.1935–1983 and E.1936–1983)
In common with almost all the other major British biscuit manufacturers, little pocket calendars, such as these Huntley & Palmers examples, were put inside selected biscuit tins each Christmas. They were never put inside 'Juvenile' tins.

CARR & CO.

M.40-1983
'JUBILEE' 1887
Transfer printed
Made by Hudson Scott & Sons for Carr & Co.
H.14cm. W.10cm. D.10cm.

M.41-1983
'PETS' c.1887
Offset litho printed
Made for Carr & Co.
H.7.2cm. W.16.2cm. D.10.2cm.

M.42-1983
'THE SNOW QUEEN' c.1890
Transfer printed with embossing
Made for Carr & Co.
H.15.3cm. W.11.9cm. D.8.2cm.

M.43-1983
'JUVENILE' c.1890
Transfer printed
Made for Carr & Co.
H.11.6cm. W.7.6cm. D.7.6cm.

M.44-1983
'JUVENILE No. 1' c.1890
Transfer printed
Made for Carr & Co. (printed label inside lid)
H.11.6cm. W.7.6cm. D.7.6cm.

M.45-1983
'CHRISTMAS TIN' 1892
Offset litho printed
Made for Carr & Co.
H.4.5cm. W.16.4cm. D.10cm.

M.46-1983
'NORWAY' c.1892
Transfer printed
Made for Carr & Co. (printed label inside lid)
H.17cm. W.11.4cm. D.11.9cm.

M.47-1983
'JUVENILE (OBLONG)' c.1892
Transfer printed
Made for Carr & Co.
H.12cm. W.8.9cm. D.6cm.

M.48-1983
'ICE MAIDEN' c.1892
Transfer printed with embossing
Made for Carr & Co. (printed label inside lid)
H.15.3cm. W.11.9cm. D.8.2cm.

M.49-1983
'ISLE OF WIGHT' c.1892
Offset litho printed
Made for Carr & Co. (printed label inside lid)
H.7.4cm. W.16.5cm. D.10cm.

M.50-1983
'JUVENILE No. 1 (SQUARE)' c.1892
Transfer printed
Made for Carr & Co. (printed label inside lid)
H.11.6cm. W.7.6cm. D.7.6cm.

M.51-1983
'SEASONS' c.1892
Transfer printed
Made for Carr & Co. (printed label inside lid)
H.14cm. W.10.2cm. D.10.2cm.

M.52-1983
'JUVENILE No. 2 (SQUARE)' c.1892
Transfer printed
Made for Carr & Co. (printed label inside lid)
H.11.6cm. W.7.6cm. D.7.6cm.

M.53-1983
'JUVENILE (NURSERY RHYMES)' 1893
Transfer printed with embossing
Made for Carr & Co.
H.11.6cm. W.7.6cm. D.7.6cm.

M.54-1983
'JUVENILE (COTTAGE)' 1894
Transfer printed
Made for Carr & Co.
H.12cm. W.8.9cm. D.6cm.

M.55-1983
'TENNYSON' 1894
Offset litho printed
Made for Carr & Co.
H.11.7cm. W.17cm. D.7.4cm.

M.56-1983
'JUVENILE No. 1' 1895
Transfer printed
Made for Carr & Co.
H.12cm. W.8.9cm. D.6cm.

M.57-1983
'JUVENILE No. 1 (MARINE)' 1896
Transfer printed
Made for Carr & Co.
H.11.7cm. W.7.6cm. D.7.6cm.

M.58-1983
'ANIMALS' 1896
Transfer printed with embossed lid
Made for Carr & Co.
H.15.6cm. W.11.9cm. D.8.1cm.

M.59-1983
'IRISH' 1896
Oval, with shaped sides
Transfer printed
Made for Carr & Co.
H.8cm. W.25.5cm. D.10.8cm.

M.60-1983
'SHELL' 1897
In the form of a shell
Offset litho printed with embossing
Made for Carr & Co.
H.8cm. W.17cm. D.16.5cm.

M.61-1983
'JUVENILE No. 2' c.1897
Transfer printed
Made for Carr & Co. (printed label inside lid)
H.11.6cm. W.7.6cm. D.7.6cm.

M.62-1983
'JUVENILE No. 1 (KITTENS)' 1897
Transfer printed
Made for Carr & Co.
H.12cm. W.8.9cm. D.6cm.

M.63-1983
'JUVENILE No. 1' c.1899
With scenes from Hans Christian Andersen's
The Marsh King's Daughter
Transfer printed
Made for Carr & Co.
H.12cm. W.8.9cm. D.6cm.

M.64-1983
'JUVENILE DROP BOX' 1899
A money box
Offset litho printed
Made for Carr & Co.
H.7.6cm. W.10cm. D.8cm.

M.65-1983
'CROWN DERBY' 1899
Octagonal
Offset litho printed
Made for Carr & Co.
H.14.5cm. W.15.3cm.

M.66-1983
'CASH BOX' (large version) 1901
A money-box with handle
Offset litho printed
Made for Carr & Co.
H.6.6cm. W.19.2cm. D.10.5cm.

M.67-1983
'KIT BAG (JUVENILE)' 1902
A simulated luggage trunk
Offset litho printed
Made for Carr & Co.
H.9.5cm. W.12.3cm. D.8.2cm.

M.68-1983
'CORONATION' 1902
Offset litho printed
Manufacturer's mark: Made by Hudson Scott
& Sons Ltd. Carlisle England
Made by Hudson Scott & Sons for Carr & Co.
H.11.3cm. W.14.3cm. D.10.5cm.

M.69-1983
'CORONATION JUVENILE' 1902
Offset litho printed
Manufacturer's mark: Made by Hudson Scott
& Sons Ltd. Carlisle England
Made by Hudson Scott & Co. for Carr & Co.
H.10.7cm. W.10.2cm. D.8.1cm.

M.70-1983
'LITTLE ROMPS' 1902
With scene of kittens on lid
Offset litho printed, with wool handles
Made for Carr & Co.
H.5cm. W.14.4cm. D.10.6cm.

M.71-1983
'EGYPTIAN GLOVE BOX' 1902
Offset litho printed
Made for Carr & Co.
H.8.3cm. W.24.5cm. D.10.4cm.

M.72-1983
'LITTLE GUARDIAN' 1903
With scenes of puppies and kittens
Offset litho printed, with wool handles
Made for Carr & Co.
H.4.3cm. W.14.3cm. D.10.5cm.

M.73-1983
'KIT BAG' 1903
A child's satchel
Offset litho printed with embossing
Made for Carr & Co.
H. 10.5cm. (excluding handle). W.13.1cm.
D.8.3cm.

M.74-1983
'KIT BAG' 1903
A child's satchel
Offset litho printed with embossing
Made for Carr & Co.
H. 10.5cm. (excluding handle). W.13.1cm.
D.8.3cm.

M.75-1983
'SWEETHEART' c.1903
A casket on feet
Offset litho printed with embossing
Made for Carr & Co.
H.14.2cm. W.20.6cm. D.9.1cm.

M.76+a-1983
'CELTIC VASE' 1905
A pair of vases
Offset litho printed (imitation oxidised silver)
with embossing
Marked: Patent No. 18593
Made by Hudson Scott & Sons for Carr & Co.
H.19cm. W.11.8cm. D.11.8cm.

M.77-1983
'GREENWOOD CASKET' 1905
A casket on feet
Offset litho printed with embossing
Made for Carr & Co.
H.14cm. W.22cm. D.12.2cm.

M.78-1983
'LIFEBOAT' 1907
A lifeboat; with its original paper lining inside
Offset litho printed
Marked: No. 8372 and 6101
Made for Carr & Co.
H.14.5cm. W.37.5cm. D.14.5cm.

M.79-1983
'WHITE STAR' 1908
Oval, with clasp; with scenes of the White Star
Steamship *Adriatic*
Offset litho printed
Manufacturer's mark: B. W. & M. Ltd.
Mansfield
Made by Barringer, Wallis & Manners for
Carr & Co.
H.4.1cm. W.17.4cm. D.9.6cm.

M.80-1983
'LADY BLESSINGTON VASE' 1911
A two-handled vase with reproductions of
Thomas Lawrence's portraits of Lady
Blessington and the Marchioness of Westminster
Offset litho printed with embossing
Made for Carr & Co.
H.19cm. W.17cm.

M.81-1983
'SCOUT' 1911
With scenes of Boy Scouts
Offset litho printed
Marked: Copyright 1166
Made by Hudson Scott & Sons for Carr & Co.
H.5.7cm. W.13.8cm. D.13.8cm.

M.82-1983
'MIRROR' 1924
Oval, with an oval mirror inset into the lid
Offset litho printed with embossing
Made for Carr & Co.
H.6cm. W.18.3cm. D.13.5cm.

M.83-1983
'ART BOX' 1924
Aluminium
Manufacturer's mark: NCJ
Made by N. C. Joseph Ltd. for Carr & Co.
Copied from a pewter box designed by
Archibald Knox c.1903
H.10.3cm. W.12cm. D.12cm.

M.84-1983
'LIFEBOAT' 1925
A wheeled toy in the form of the lifeboat
Grace Darling
Offset litho printed
Manufacturer's mark: Hudson Scott & Son Ltd.
Carlisle, England
Made by Hudson Scott & Sons for Carr & Co.
H.11cm. L.25cm.

M.85-1983
'GOLDEN CASKET' 1926
Offset litho printed with embossing, with scene
from *Cinderella* on the lid
Made for Carr & Co.
H.7.5cm. W.17cm. D.12cm.

M.86-1983
'DICE CASKET' 1929
With mechanical dice game inset into lid, and its
original cardboard box
Offset litho printed
Made for Carr & Co.
H.8cm. W.15.5cm. D.11.7cm.

M.87-1983
'CHARIOT RACE' 1936
With a reproduction of Prof. Alex Wagner's
painting *The Chariot Race* on the lid
Offset litho printed
Made by Hudson Scott & Sons for Carr & Co.
H.5.5cm. W.23cm. D.11.5cm.

M.88-1983
'TEA CADDY' 1936
Semicircular, simulating inlaid wood, with a
reproduction of J. B. Greuze's painting
The Milk Maid
Offset litho printed
Marked: 1929
Made by Hudson Scott & Sons for Carr & Co.
H.14.5cm. W.18cm. D.9cm.

M.89-1983
'HIGHLAND' 1936
Offset litho printed
Marked: 1928
Made by Barringer, Wallis & Manners for
Carr & Co.
H.5cm. W.24.5cm. D.10.5cm.

M.90-1983
CORONATION 1937
Offset litho printed
Made for Carr & Co.
H.6cm. W.20cm. D.11.8cm.

M.91-1983
'DORSET' 1937
With a view of Thomas Hardy's birthplace on
the lid
Offset litho printed
Marked: 1985
Made by Barringer, Wallis & Manners for
Carr & Co.
H.5cm. W.24.5cm. D.10.5cm.

M.92-1983
'LILY' 1937
Offset litho printed
Made for Carr & Co.
H.7.3cm. W.21.2cm. D.13.3cm.

CO-OPERATIVE WHOLESALE SOCIETY

M.93-1983
MARJORY MAY c.1887
Transfer printed
Manufacturer's mark: Hudson Scott & Sons,
Carlisle
Made by Hudson Scott & Sons for Co-Operative
Wholesale Society
H.14.5cm. W.10cm. D.10cm.

M.94-1983
PETS c.1890
Offset litho printed
Made for Co-Operative Wholesale Society
H.12cm. W.7.8cm. D.7.8cm.

M.95-1983
ISLE OF MAN c.1890
Transfer printed
Made for Co-Operative Wholesale Society
H.14.5cm. W.10cm. D.10cm.

M.96-1983
BISCUITS c.1900
Offset litho printed
Made for Co-Operative Wholesale Society
H.7.5cm. W.24.5cm. D.10.5cm.

M.97-1983
'CRUMPSALL WORKS' c.1901
With a view of C.W.S. factory at Crumpsall on
the lid
Offset litho printed
Manufacturer's mark: Hudson Scott & Sons
Ltd., Carlisle
Made by Hudson Scott & Sons for Co-Operative
Wholesale Society
H.6cm. W.14.2cm. D.10.5cm.

M.98-1983
'TRUNK' c.1901
A luggage trunk
Offset litho printed
Marked: Registered
Made by Hudson Scott & Sons for Co-Operative
Wholesale Society
H.9cm. W.12.3cm. D.8cm.

M.99-1983
MUSIC CASKET c.1904
A casket on ball feet
Offset litho printed
Made by Barringer, Wallis & Manners for
Co-Operative Wholesale Society
H.11.5cm. W.18cm. D.11.5cm.

M.100-1983
GERANIUM c.1904
A casket with handle
Offset litho printed
Made by Barringer, Wallis & Manners for
Co-Operative Wholesale Society
H.14cm. W.19.3cm. D.9.4cm.

M.101-1983
'SAFE' 1908
A safe with handle
Offset litho printed with embossing
Made for Co-Operative Wholesale Society
H.11.8cm. W.9.5cm. D.7.4cm.

M.102-1983
'PUSS' c.1909
Oval. Wool handles missing
Offset litho printed
Made by Hudson Scott & Sons for Co-Operative
Wholesale Society
H.11cm. W.14cm. D.9cm.

M.103-1983
'SWALLOWS' 1910
Offset litho printed with embossed lid
Made for Co-Operative Wholesale Society
H.6.1cm. W.19.2cm. D.7.3cm.

M.104-1983
NESTING c.1911
Offset litho printed
Made for Co-Operative Wholesale Society
H.6cm. W.16.9cm. D.16.9cm.

M.105-1983
'GIPSY VAN' 1912
A wheeled toy
Offset litho printed
Made by Hudson Scott & Sons for Co-Operative
Wholesale Society
H.12cm. W.14.4cm. D.8cm.

M.106-1983
'BLUE BIRD' 1912
A bird
Offset litho printed with embossing
Made by Barringer, Wallis & Manners for
Co-Operative Wholesale Society (printed label
inside lid)
H.23.5cm.

M.107-1983
'MORLAND GLOVE BOX' 1912
Curved front edge; with a reproduction of a
painting by George Morland on the lid
Offset litho printed
Made by Barringer, Wallis & Manners for
Co-Operative Wholesale Society
H.6.2cm. W.26cm. D.13cm.

M.108-1983
'POSTAL PILLAR' 1913
An oval pillar-box
Offset litho printed with embossing
Made by Barringer, Wallis & Manners for
Co-Operative Wholesale Society
H.12.8cm. W.11.5cm. D.6.5cm.

M.109-1983
'SIGNAL BOX' 1914
A signal box
Offset litho printed
Manufacturer's mark: Hudson Scott & Sons,
Carlisle, England
Made by Hudson Scott & Sons for Co-Operative
Wholesale Society
H.13.5cm. W.10cm. D.6.2cm.

M.110-1983
ROMAN FEAST c.1914
Offset litho printed
Made for Co-Operative Wholesale Society
H.6.5cm. W.21cm. D.19cm.

M.111-1983
'WINDERMERE HANDKERCHIEF BOX'
1915
Offset litho printed
Manufacturer's mark: Hudson Scott & Sons
Ltd., Carlisle, England
Made by Hudson Scott & Sons for Co-Operative
Wholesale Society
H.5cm. W.13.3cm. D.13.3cm.

M112 and a-1983
URN c.1920
A pair of two-handled vases
Offset litho printed with embossing
Made for Co-Operative Wholesale Society
H.23.5cm. W.11.5cm.

M113-1983
HANDKERCHIEF BOX c.1923
Offset litho printed
Made for Co-Operative Wholesale Society
H.6cm. W.17.8cm. D.17.8cm.

M114-1983
MISTLETOE c.1924
Offset litho printed
Made by Barringer, Wallis & Manners for
Co-Operative Wholesale Society
H.5cm. W.13.5cm. D.13.5cm.

M115-1983
OLDEN TIMES c.1924
With a scene of The King's Head, Chigwell,
on the lid; shaped corners
Offset litho printed
Made by Barringer, Wallis & Manners for
Co-Operative Wholesale Society
H.8.5cm. W.18.1cm. D.13cm.

M116-1983
HORSE SHOE c.1925
In the shape of a horseshoe
Offset litho printed
Made by Barringer, Wallis & Manners for
Co-Operative Wholesale Society
H.4.6cm. W.13.5cm. D.14.4cm.

M117-1983
SCALES c.1925
With a pair of scales on top of the lid
Offset litho printed
Marked: No.10130
Made by Barringer, Wallis & Manners for
Co-Operative Wholesale Society
H.6.3cm. W.17.2cm. D.7.5cm.
(measurements excluding scales)

M118-1983
PILLAR BOX c.1926
A money-box in the form of an oval pillar-box
Offset litho printed
Made by Hudson Scott & Sons for
Co-Operative Wholesale Society
H.16.5cm. W.11.5cm. D.5.5cm.

M119-1983
FIRESIDE c.1927
Offset litho printed
Made by Hudson Scott & Sons for
Co-Operative Wholesale Society
H.6.8cm. W.12.2cm. D.9.1cm.

M120-1983
'FLORENTINE' 1930
Copper plated, with embossing
Made by Barringer, Wallis & Manners for
Co-Operative Wholesale Society
H.8cm. W.24.5cm. D.12.6cm.

M121-1983
'GOLDEN JAR' 1930
A jar on three feet
Sprayed in imitation of gold, with embossing
Made by Barringer, Wallis & Manners for
Co-Operative Wholesale Society
H.15.2cm. D.13.5cm.

M122-1983
'BALLOONS' 1930
Offset litho printed
Made by Hudson Scott & Sons for
Co-Operative Wholesale Society
H.7cm. W.14.2cm. D.8.7cm.

M.123-1983
'PRIMROSES' 1930
Oval
Offset litho printed
Made by Hudson Scott & Sons for
Co-Operative Wholesale Society
H.6.8cm. W.17.3cm. D.10.5cm.

M.124-1983
INDIAN BOX c.1930
Offset litho printed
Made for Co-Operative Wholesale Society
H.4.8cm. W.16.7cm. D.11.2cm.

M.125-1983
'MOONLIGHT' 1932
Oval
Offset litho printed
Made by Barringer, Wallis & Manners for
Co-Operative Society
H.7.7cm. W.22.3cm. D.12.7cm.

M.126-1983
'GLEANERS' 1932
With reproductions of J. F. Millet's paintings
The Gleaners and Angelus
Offset litho printed
Manufacturer's mark: B. W. & M. Ltd.
Mansfield No.14166. Made in England
Made by Barringer, Wallis & Manners for
Co-Operative Wholesale Society
H.15.5cm. W.11.6cm. D.11.6cm.

M.127-1983
'MORLAND CASKET' 1932
Offset litho printed, with brass lid with
embossed reproduction of a painting by
George Morland
Made by Barringer, Wallis & Manners for
Co-Operative Wholesale Society
H.6.6cm. W.21.3cm. D.11.2cm.

M.128-1983
'CHILDREN'S TALES' 1933
Offset litho printed
Made by Hudson Scott & Sons for
Co-Operative Wholesale Society
H.11.2cm. W.10.8cm. D.6.7cm.

M.129-1983
'CARD PARTY' 1933
Offset litho printed
Manufacturer's mark: Hudson Scott & Sons
Ltd. Carlisle, England
Made by Hudson Scott & Sons for
Co-Operative Wholesale Society
H.4.5cm. W.15cm. D.12.7cm.

M.130-1983
'HAVEN' 1934
Octagonal
Offset litho printed
Manufacturer's mark: B. W. & M. Ltd.
Mansfield No.15926. Made in England.
Copyright
Made by Barringer, Wallis & Manners for
Co-Operative Wholesale Society
H.6cm. W.13.9cm.

M.131-1983
'COMO' 1935
Offset litho printed
Manufacturer's mark: Hudson Scott & Sons
Ltd. Carlisle, England
Made by Hudson Scott & Sons for
Co-Operative Wholesale Society
H.3.9cm. W.21cm. D.11.5cm.

M.132-1983
SILVER JUBILEE 1935
Oval
Offset litho printed
Made for Co-Operative Wholesale Society
H.4cm. W.29.9cm. D.20.6cm.

M.133-1983
'INNOCENCE' 1937
With a reproduction of Lancret's painting
Innocence on the lid
Offset litho printed
Made for Co-Operative Wholesale Society
H.6.5cm. W.18.4cm. D.9.8cm.

Wm. CRAWFORD & SONS

M.134-1983
URCHINS c.1890
Transfer printed
Made for Wm. Crawford & Sons
H.14.8cm. W.10.2cm. D.10.2cm.

M.135-1983
GIRLS OF THE PERIOD c.1893
Crescent-shaped
Transfer printed with embossing
Made by Barringer, Wallis & Manners for
Wm. Crawford & Sons
H.14.8cm. W.11.6cm. D.9.7cm.

M.136-1983
'COACHING' c.1896
With curved sides and corners
Offset litho printed with embossed lid
Manufacturer's mark: Hudson Scott & Sons
Carlisle
Made by Hudson Scott & Sons for Wm.
Crawford & Sons
H.10cm. W.14.5cm. D.12.6cm.

M.137-1983
'IVORY CASKET' 1910
A casket with handle
Offset litho printed and embossed with figures
after A. Dürer
Marked: Rd. 560110
Designed by Paul Greville Hudson
(1876-1960)
Made by Hudson Scott & Sons for Wm.
Crawford & Sons
H.16cm. W.16.5cm. D.11cm.

M.138 and a- 1983
'RUSSIAN JUG' 1911
Pair of lidded jugs
Offset litho printed with incised decoration
Marked: Regd. No.577692
Made by Barringer, Wallis & Manners for
Wm. Crawford & Sons
H.25.5cm. W.13.2cm.

M.139-1983
'CHUMS' 1911
Offset litho printed with embossing
Marked: Regd. No. 579332
Made by Barringer, Wallis & Manners for
Wm. Crawford & Sons
H.24.8cm. W.11.4cm. D.7.8cm.

M.140-1983
'MENAGERIE' 1911
A wheeled circus cage filled with animals
Offset litho printed
Marked: Regd. No. 580291
Made by Hudson Scott & Sons for Wm.
Crawford & Sons
H.11.7cm. W.14.3cm. D.8cm.

M.141-1983
'HURDY GURDY' 1912
A wheeled toy
Offset litho printed with embossing
Marked: Regd. No. 594837
Made by Barringer, Wallis & Manners for
Wm. Crawford & Sons
H.16cm. W.14cm. D.7.7cm.

M.142-1983
'TEA TIME BOX' 1913
Simulating wood
Offset litho printed
Made for Wm. Crawford & Sons
H.15.3cm. W.16cm. D.10cm.

M.143-1983
'TORTOISESHELL CASKET' 1914
Offset litho printed
Made by Barringer, Wallis & Manners for
Wm. Crawford & Sons
H.10.5cm. W.21.5cm. D.12.2cm.

M.144-1983
'KASHMIR CASKET' 1914
With curved sides, and knob
Offset litho printed
Made for Wm. Crawford & Sons
H.10cm. (including knob) W.23.6cm.
D.11.5cm.

M.145-1983
'ARCADIA VASE' 1919
A three-handled vase with knob
Offset litho printed with embossing
Made for Wm. Crawford & Sons
H.19.3cm. Diam.12.5cm.

M.146-1983
'GOLDEN CASKET' 1925
A casket on feet
Sprayed in imitation of gold with embossed
decoration
Made for Wm. Crawford & Sons
H.11cm. W.22.3cm. D.12cm. (maximum
dimensions)

M.147-1983
'LIZARD SKIN CASKET' 1926
A simulated lizard skin casket on feet
Offset litho printed
Made for Wm. Crawford & Sons
H.8.5cm. W.17.5cm. D.15.4cm.

M.148-1983
'SUNDIAL' 1926
A sundial
Offset litho printed
Made for Wm. Crawford & Sons
H.24cm. (including pointer) W.11.8cm.
D.11.8cm.

M.149-1983
'STAGECOACH' 1927
A wheeled toy
Offset litho printed
Made for Wm. Crawford & Sons
H.15.8cm. W.29cm. (with shaft extended)
D.9.2cm.

M.150-1983
'ATLANTIC LINER' 1927
In the form of Cunard Liner 'Berengaria'
Made for Wm. Crawford & Sons
H.11cm. L.37.8cm. W.6cm.

M.151-1983
'KASHMIR CASKET' 1928
Offset litho printed
Made for Wm. Crawford & Sons
H.7cm. W.21.1cm. D.14.7cm.

M.152-1983
'ANTIQUE TEA CADDY' 1928
Hexagonal, simulating inlaid wood
Offset litho printed
Made for Wm. Crawford & Sons
H.14.5cm. W.15.6cm. D.9.9cm.

M.153-1983
'MOTHER-OF-PEARL TRINKET BOX'
1928
Offset litho printed
Made for Wm. Crawford & Sons
H.3.5cm. W.21.4cm. D.13.8cm.

M.154-1983
'PEARL AND IVORY TRINKET BOX'
1929
Offset litho printed with embossing
Made for Wm. Crawford & Sons
H.6.5cm. W.24.6cm. D.15.1cm.

M.155-1983
'MORLAND CASKET' 1930
With shaped corners, and a reproduction of a
painting by George Morland on the lid
Offset litho printed with embossed lid
Made for Wm. Crawford & Sons
H.7cm. W.19cm. D.19cm.

M.156-1983
'LEATHERCRAFT STATIONERY BOX'
1932
With a reproduction of Fragonard's painting
The Schoolmistress on the curved lid
Offset litho printed
Made for Wm. Crawford & Sons
H.18.2cm. W.17.8cm. D.7.7cm.

M.157-1983
'WEDGWOOD CASKET' 1932
A simulated Wedgwood Jasperware casket on
feet
Offset litho printed with embossing
Made for Wm. Crawford & Sons
H.10cm. W.23.8cm. D.12.4cm.

M.158-1983
'BIKKY HOUSE' 1933
The lid of the house in the form of a money-box
Offset litho printed
Designed by Mabel Lucie Atwell (1879-1964)
Made by Barringer, Wallis & Manners for
Wm. Crawford & Sons
H.17.5cm. W.19.6cm. D.10.5cm.

M.159-1983
'MENAGERIE' 1933
A wheeled circus caravan with animals inside
Offset litho printed
Made by Barringer, Wallis & Manners for
Wm. Crawford & Sons
H.12cm. W.15.8cm. D.7.2cm.

M.160-1983
'TREASURE BOX' 1934
Offset litho printed with embossing
Made for Wm. Crawford & Sons
H.9.5cm. W.19.2cm. D.9.7cm.

M.161-1983
'FAIRY HOUSE' 1934
With money-box in lid
Offset litho printed
Designed by Mabel Lucie Atwell (1879-1964)
Made by Barringer, Wallis & Manners for
Wm. Crawford & Sons
H.20cm. Diam. 18.5cm.

M.162-1983
'FAIRY TREE' 1935
With money-box in conical lid
Offset litho printed
Marked: Reg. design no. 803235
Designed by Mabel Lucie Atwell (1879-1964)
Made by Barringer, Wallis & Manners for
Wm. Crawford & Sons
H.36cm. Diam. 15.5cm.

M.163-1983
'TEA CADDY' 1935
Offset litho printed in imitation of Rowley
Gallery inlaid wood pictures
Made by Barringer, Wallis & Manners for
Wm. Crawford & Sons
H.16.5cm. W.13cm. D.9.7cm.

M.164-1983
'MUSKETEER' 1936
With a reproduction after Meissonnier's
painting *A Musketeer* on the lid; shaped sides
Offset litho printed
Made for Wm. Crawford & Sons
H.6.3cm. W.25.6cm. D.16.6cm.

M.165-1983
'MACAW' 1936
With shaped sides
Offset litho printed
Made by Barringer, Wallis & Manners for
Wm. Crawford & Sons
H.6.4cm. W.24.7cm. D.18.2cm.

M.166-1983
'KASHMIR TEA CADDY' 1936
Offset litho printed
Made by Barringer, Wallis & Manners for
Wm. Crawford & Sons
H.17.4cm. W.13.9cm. D.9.8cm.

M.167-1983
'WALNUT TEA CADDY' 1937
Diamond-shaped; simulating inlaid walnut wood
Offset litho printed
Made by Barringer, Wallis & Manners for
Wm. Crawford & Sons
H.17.7cm. W.15cm. D.11.5cm.

M.168-1983
CORONATION 1937
With photographs of George VI and Queen
Elizabeth on the lid
Offset litho printed
Made for Wm. Crawford & Sons
H.8.5cm. W.25cm. D.9cm.

M.169-1983
CORONATION 1937
With a photograph of George VI, Queen
Elizabeth, and Princesses Elizabeth and
Margaret after Marcus Adams on the lid
Offset litho printed
Made for Wm. Crawford & Sons
H.7cm. Diam. 16.2cm.

M.170-1983
'GLOBE' 1938
A globe on a stand, in its original cardboard box
Offset litho printed
Made by Barringer, Wallis & Manners for
Wm. Crawford & Sons
H.21cm. Diam. of base 11cm.

M.171-1983
'SATINWOOD TEA CADDY' 1938
Offset litho printed
Made for Wm. Crawford & Sons
H.12.2cm. W.15.3cm. D.9cm.

M.172-1983
'CROWN DERBY' 1939
Offset litho printed
Manufacturer's mark: 6 MB Container. Made
in England
Made by Metal Box for Wm. Crawford & Sons
H.9.3cm. D.11.3cm.

M.173-1983
'HOUSE OF KNOWLEDGE' 1939
With money-box in lid. Monthly horoscope
cards missing from slots on side
Offset litho printed
Made by Barringer, Wallis & Manners for
Wm. Crawford & Sons
H.16cm. W.19.5cm. D.11.7cm.

M.174-1983
'GOLDEN TEA CADDY' 1939
Offset litho printed
Made for Wm. Crawford & Sons
H.16.4cm. W.12.7cm. D.9.5cm.

GRAY, DUNN & CO.

M.175-1983
HADDON HALL c.1890
Offset litho printed
Made for Gray, Dunn & Co.
H.7.5cm. W.18.5cm. D.12.8cm.

M.176-1983
BURNS c.1891
Offset litho printed
Made for Gray, Dunn & Co. (printed label
inside lid)
H.8.1cm. W.18.5cm. D.13cm.

M.177-1983
'SHAKESPEARE' 1892
Offset litho printed
Made for Gray, Dunn & Co.
H.8.8cm. W.18.5cm. D.12.6cm.

M.178-1983
'HOME SWEET HOME' c.1892
Hexagonal; with scenes inspired by the ballad
by Sir Henry Bishop
Offset litho printed
Made by Barringer, Wallis & Manners for
Gray, Dunn & Co.
H.15.4cm. W.13.8cm. D.8.4cm.

M.179-1983
'LAKE' 1896
Transfer-printed with embossing
Made for Gray, Dunn & Co.
H.14cm. Diam.12.5cm.

M.180-1983
'ROYALTY' 1901
Offset litho printed
Manufacturer's mark: B. W. & M. Ltd.
Mansfield
Made by Barringer, Wallis & Manners for
Gray, Dunn & Co.
H.7cm. W.13cm. D.10.5cm.

M.181-1983
'JAPANESE' c.1902
With handle and ball feet
Offset litho printed
Manufacturer's mark: Hudson Scott & Sons
Ltd. Carlisle Rd. 581911
Designed by Paul Greville Hudson (1876-1960)
Made by Hudson Scott & Sons for Gray, Dunn
& Co.
H.17.5cm. (including handle) W.11.5cm.
D.11.5cm.

M.182-1983
'CONCERTINA' 1902
Hexagonal
Offset litho printed with embossing
Made by Barringer, Wallis & Manners for
Gray, Dunn & Co.
H.9.8cm. W.10.5cm.

M.183-1983
'ART SILVER GLOVE BOX' 1903
Offset litho printed and imitation oxidised
silver, with embossing
Manufacturer's mark: B. W. & M. Ltd.
Mansfield
Made by Barringer, Wallis & Manners for
Gray, Dunn & Co.
H.5.5cm. W.31cm. D.9.5cm.

M.184-1983
'POST OFFICE' 1904
Offset litho printed with embossing
Made by Barringer, Wallis & Manners for
Gray, Dunn & Co.
H.13.5cm. W.10.1cm. D.6.4cm.

M.185-1983
'SEE-SAW' 1905
Crescent-shaped; with scenes of a boy on a
rocking horse, and children on a see-saw
Offset litho printed with embossing
Made by Barringer, Wallis & Manners for
Gray, Dunn & Co.
H.12.2cm. W.16cm. D.6cm.

M.186-1983
'ROSES' 1906
A vase
Offset litho printed
Made by Barringer, Wallis & Manners for
Gray, Dunn & Co.
H.16.5cm. W.13cm. D.13cm.

M.187-1983
'GEORGE MORLAND CASKET' 1910
With a reproduction of a painting by George
Morland on the lid; curved front edge
Offset litho printed
Marked: Regd. no. 579320
Made by Barringer, Wallis & Manners for
Gray, Dunn & Co.
H.6.2cm. W.26cm. D.13cm.

M.188-1983
OUR DARLINGS c.1913
Rectangular bed with bedhead, with two
children asleep
Offset litho printed
Made by Barringer, Wallis & Manners for
Gray, Dunn & Co.
H.8.8cm. W.16.7cm. D.8.2cm.

M.189-1983
'RACING MOTOR CAR' c.1926
A wheeled racing car
Offset litho printed
Marked: No.11060
Made by Barringer, Wallis & Manners
(Burnet Ltd.) for Gray, Dunn & Co.
L.24.5cm. H.10.5cm.

HUNTLEY & PALMERS

M.190-1983
BEN GEORGE 1868
Transfer-printed
Marked: Ben. George Patentee London
Transfer designed by Owen Jones (1809-1874)
and made by Benjamin George George
Box made by Huntley & Boorne for Huntley &
Palmers
H.5cm. W.21.8cm. D.8.7cm.

M.191-1983
COURT c.1870
Transfer-printed; the picture on the lid of a
girl and puppy printed on thin cardboard and
pasted on
Marked: Ben. George Patentee. Hatton Gardens
London E.C.
Transfer made by Benjamin George George
Box made by Huntley & Boorne for Huntley &
Palmers
H.8.7cm. W.16.5cm. D.11.5cm.

M.192-1983
COURT c.1870
Transfer-printed; the picture of roses on the lid
printed on thin cardboard and pasted on
Marked: Ben. George Patentee London
Transfer made by Benjamin George George
Box made by Huntley & Boorne for Huntley &
Palmers
H.8.7cm. W.16.5cm. D.11.5cm.

M.193-1983
COURT c.1870
Transfer-printed; the picture of flowers on the
lid printed on thin cardboard and pasted on
Marked: Ben. George. Patentee. London
Transfer made by Benjamin George George
Box made by Huntley & Boorne for Huntley &
Palmers
H.8.7cm. W.16.5cm. D.11.5cm.

M.194-1983
EMBOSSED COURT c.1871
Transfer-printed and embossed
Transfer made by Benjamin George George
Box made by Huntley & Boorne for Huntley &
Palmers
H.8.7cm. W.16.5cm. D.11.5cm.

M.195-1983
FACTORY PICTURE c.1873
Direct printed
Made by Huntley, Boorne & Stevens for
Huntley & Palmers
H.8.7cm. W.16.5cm. D.11.5cm

M.196-1983
FACTORY PICTURE c.1873
Direct printed
Made by Huntley, Boorne & Stevens for
Huntley & Palmers
H.7cm. W.16.8cm. D.11.5cm.

M.197-1983
'TRAVELLERS' c.1873
A sliding cylinder
Direct printed
Made by Huntley, Boorne & Stevens for
Huntley & Palmers
L.34.7cm.   Diam.7.6cm.

M.198-1983
COURT c.1880
Decorated with butterflies and with Royal
Coat of Arms on lid
Offset litho printed
Marked: E & Ms Pat
Made by Huntley, Boorne & Stevens for
Huntley & Palmers
H.8.7cm.   W.16.5cm.   D.11.5cm.

M.199-1983
SMALL SPECIALITY c.1880
Decorated with lilies and with Royal Coat of
Arms on lid; with original cut and embossed
paper label by Mansell, London, inside lid.
Offset litho printed
Marked: B & Ms Pat
Made by Huntley, Boorne & Stevens for
Huntley & Palmers
H.4.5cm.   W.15.3cm.   D.9.5cm.

M.200-1983
SMALL SPECIALITY c.1880
Decorated with lilies and with Royal Coat of
Arms on lid
Offset litho printed
Marked: B & Ms Pat
Made by Huntley, Boorne & Stevens for
Huntley & Palmers
H.4.5cm.   W.15.3cm.   D.9.5cm.

M.201-1983
ORNAMENTAL (OBLONG) c.1880
Decorated with Royal Coat of Arms and
Factory name on lid
Offset litho printed
Marked: B & Ms Pat
Made by Huntley, Boorne & Stevens for
Huntley & Palmers
H.5cm.   W.21.8cm.   D.8.7cm.

M.202-1983
SMALL SPECIALITY (MULTI
COLOURED) c.1880
Offset litho printed
Marked: B & Ms Pat
Made by Huntley, Boorne & Stevens for
Huntley & Palmers
H.4.5cm.   W.15.3cm.   D.9.5cm.

M.203-1983
LARGE SPECIALITY (BLUE) c.1880
Offset litho printed
Marked: B & Ms Pat
Made by Huntley, Boorne & Stevens for
Huntley & Palmers
H.7.7cm.   W.18cm.   D.11.3cm.

M.204-1983
OBLONG SPECIALITY (BLUE) c.1880
Offset litho printed
Made by Huntley, Boorne & Stevens for
Huntley & Palmers
H.5cm.   W.21.8cm   D.8.7cm.

M.205-1983
CHRISTMAS BISCUITS c.1880
Offset litho printed
Made by Huntley, Boorne & Stevens for
Huntley & Palmers
H.9.5cm.   W.19.8cm.   D.13.5cm.

M.206-1983
'SEASONS' (GOLD) c.1884
Offset litho printed
Marked: B & Ms Pat
Made by Huntley, Boorne & Stevens for
Huntley & Palmers
H.5cm   W.21.8cm.   D.8.7cm.

M.207-1983
'SEASONS' (BEIGE) c.1884
Offset litho printed
Marked: B & Ms Pat
Made by Huntley, Boorne & Stevens for
Huntley & Palmers
H.5cm   W.21.8cm.   D.8.7cm.

M.208-1983
'SEASONS' (YELLOW) c.1884
Offset litho printed
Marked: B & Ms Pat
Made by Huntley, Boorne & Stevens for
Huntley & Palmers
H.5cm.   W.21.8cm.   D.8.7cm.

M.209-1983
'BRAEMAR' 1886
Offset litho printed
Marked: B & Ms Pat
Made by Huntley, Boorne & Stevens for
Huntley & Palmers
H.14cm.   W.10cm.   D.10cm.

M.210-1983
'FESTAL' 1887
With lines from a poem by M. Howitt
Offset litho printed
Marked L E & Ms Pat
Made by Huntley, Boorne & Stevens for
Huntley & Palmers
H.5.7cm.   W.21.3cm.   D.8cm.

M.211-1983
'ORIENT' 1887
With shaped ends
Offset litho printed
Marked: B & Ms Pat
Made by Huntley, Boorne & Stevens for
Huntley & Palmers
H.7cm.   W.24.3cm.

M.212-1983
'VENICE' 1887
With shaped sides and reproduction of a
painting by W. Goodall on the lid
Offset litho printed
Marked: B & Ms Pat
Made by Huntley, Boorne & Stevens for
Huntley & Palmers
H.9cm.   W.20cm.   D.13.3cm.

M.213-1983
'BARONIAL HALL' 1887
With shaped sides
Offset litho printed
Marked: B & Ms Pat
Made by Huntley, Boorne & Stevens for
Huntley & Palmers
H.9cm.   W.20cm.   D.13.3cm.

M.214-1983
GOLDEN JUBILEE 1887
Offset litho printed
Marked: E & Ms Pat
Made by Huntley, Boorne & Stevens for
Huntley & Palmers
H.8.8cm.   W.13.5cm.   D.13.5cm.

M.215-1983
UNIVERSAL c.1887
With shaped sides
Offset litho printed
Marked: B & Ms Pat
Made by Huntley, Boorne & Stevens for
Huntley & Palmers
H.9cm.   W.20cm.   D.13.3cm.

M.216-1983
'WILDFLOWER' 1887
With shaped ends
Offset litho printed
Marked: B & Ms Pat
Made by Huntley, Boorne & Stevens for
Huntley & Palmers
H.8.2cm.   W.18cm.   D.11.3cm.

M.217-1983
'FEAST OF ROSES' 1888
With shaped sides
Offset litho printed
Marked: B & Ms Pat
Made by Huntley, Boorne & Stevens for
Huntley & Palmers
H.9cm.   W.20cm.   D.13.3cm.

M.218-1983
'OLDEN TIMES' 1888
Oval, with shaped sides
Offset litho printed
Marked: B & Ms Pat
Made by Huntley, Boorne & Stevens for
Huntley & Palmers
H.9.5cm   W.18.5cm.   D.12.7cm.

M.219-1983
'WAGON' 1888
Oval, with shaped sides
Offset litho printed
Marked: B & Ms Pat
Made by Huntley, Boorne & Stevens for
Huntley & Palmers
H.9.5cm.   W.18.5cm.   D.12.7cm.

M.220-1983
'COACH & HORSES' 1888
With curved sides
Offset litho printed
Marked: B & Ms Pat
Made by Huntley, Boorne & Stevens for
Huntley & Palmers
H.9.3cm.   W.16.5cm.   D.12.2cm.

M.221-1983
'WINTER SCENERY' 1888
With curved sides
Offset litho printed
Marked: B & Ms Pat
Made by Huntley, Boorne & Stevens for
Huntley & Palmers
H.9.3cm.   W.16.5cm.   D.12.2cm.

M.222-1983
'FOUR IN HAND' 1888
With curved ends
Offset litho printed
Marked: B & Ms Pat
Made by Huntley, Boorne & Stevens for
Huntley & Palmers
H.5cm.   W.15.2cm.   D.9.5cm.

M.223-1983
'AGRICULTURAL LIFE' c.1888
Oval, with shaped sides
Offset litho printed
Marked: B & Ms Pat
Made by Huntley, Boorne & Stevens for
Huntley & Palmers
H.9.2cm.   W.18.1cm.   D13.8cm.

M.224-1983
'SAILOR' 1888
Offset litho printed
Marked: B & Ms Pat
Made by Huntley, Boorne & Stevens for
Huntley & Palmers
H.16cm.   W.13.5cm.   D.13.5cm.

M.225-1983
'SPORTING' 1889
Oval, with shaped sides
Offset litho printed
Marked: B & Ms Pat
Made by Huntley, Boorne & Stevens for
Huntley & Palmers
H.9.2cm.   W.18.1cm.   D.13.8cm.

M.226-1983
'FARM' 1889
With shaped ends
Offset litho printed
Marked: B & Ms Pat
Made by Huntley, Boorne & Stevens for
Huntley & Palmers
H.8.2cm.   W.18cm.   D.11.3cm.

M.227-1983
'FESTAL' 1889
Offset litho printed
Marked: B & Ms Pat
Made by Huntley, Boorne & Stevens for
Huntley & Palmers
H.5.7cm.   W.21.3cm.   D.8cm.

M.228-1983
'HUNTING' c.1889
With shaped corners
Offset litho printed
Marked: B & Ms Pat
Made by Huntley, Boorne & Stevens for
Huntley & Palmers
H.9.3cm.   W.16.5cm.   D.12.5cm.

M.229-1983
'LANDSCAPE' c.1890
With shaped corners
Offset litho printed
Marked: B & Ms Pat
Made by Huntley, Boorne & Stevens for
Huntley & Palmers
H.9.3cm.   W.16.5cm.   D12.5cm.

M.230-1983
'SEASIDE' 1890
Offset litho printed
Marked: B & Ms Pat
Made by Huntley, Boorne & Stevens for
Huntley & Palmers
H.16cm.   W.13.5cm.   D.13.5cm.

M.231-1983
'POLO' 1890
Oval
Offset litho printed
Marked: B & Ms Pat
Made by Huntley, Boorne & Stevens for
Huntley & Palmers
H.10cm.   W.18.4cm.   D.14.5cm.

M.232-1983
'PHEASANT' 1890
Offset litho printed
Marked : B & Ms Pat
Made by Huntley, Boorne & Stevens for
Huntley & Palmers
H.8cm.   D.16cm.

M.233-1983
'FIRESIDE' c.1890
With scenes of children
Offset litho printed with embossing
Marked : B & Ms Pat
Made by Huntley, Boorne & Stevens for
Huntley & Palmers
H.14.5cm.   W.10.2cm.   D.10.2cm.

M.234-1983
'FOREST' 1891
Four-leaf clover-shaped
Offset litho printed
Made by Huntley, Boorne & Stevens for
Huntley & Palmers
H.15.8cm.   W14.5cm.   D.14.5cm.

M.235-1983
'ARABIAN' 1891
A casket
Offset litho printed
Made for Huntley & Palmers
H.10cm.   W.21cm.   D.13cm.

M.236-1983
'PASTORAL' 1891
Offset litho printed
Made for Huntley & Palmers
H.8cm.   Diam.16cm.

M.237-1983
'OLYMPIAN' 1892
With shaped sides
Offset litho printed
Made for Huntley & Palmers
H.9cm.   W.17.5cm.   D.12.1cm.

M.238-1983
'ATHLETIC' 1892
Triangular
Offset litho printed
Made for Huntley & Palmers
H.11cm.   W.14cm.

M.239-1983
'FIRE BRIGADE' 1892
Four-leaf clover -shaped
Offset litho printed
Made for Huntley & Palmers
H.15.8cm.   W.14.5cm.   D.14.5cm.

M.240-1983
'FISHERMEN' 1892
Hexagonal
Offse litho printed
Made for Huntely & Palmers
H.15.4cm.   W.14cm.   D.8.4cm.

M.241-1983
'COMPANIONS' 1892
With shaped ends
Offset litho printed
Made for Huntley & Palmers (for export)
H.8.2cm.   W.18cm.   D.11.3cm.

M.242-1983
'OAK' 1892
With catch fastening ; simulating wood
Offset litho printed
Made for Huntley & Palmers (for export)
H.4.5cm.   W.15.3cm.   D.9.6cm.

M.243-1983
'SWAN CASKET' 1892
A casket
Offset litho printed
Made for Huntley & Palmers
H.10cm.   W.21cm.   D.13cm.

M.244-1983
'ROBINSON CRUSOE' 1892
Hexagonal
Offset litho printed
Made for Huntley & Palmers
H.15.4cm.   W.14cm.   D.11.3cm.

M.245-1983
'HARMONY' 1893
Quatrefoil-shaped ; with musical scenes
Offset litho printed
Made for Huntley & Palmers
H.9.3cm.   W.17.4cm.   D.16.6cm.

M.246-1983
'VILLAGE BLACKSMITH' 1893
Triangular
Offset litho printed
Made for Huntley & Palmers
H.11cm.   W.14cm.

M.247-1983
'TORTOISESHELL' 1893
With shaped sides
Offset litho printed
Made for Huntley & Palmers
H.5.8cm.   W.22cm.   D.8.7cm

M.248-1983
'GIPSY' 1893
Semi-circular, with shaped sides
Offset litho printed
Made for Huntley & Palmers
H.15.2cm.   W.14.4cm.   D.8.6cm.

M.249-1983
'OLDEN TIMES' 1893
Semi-circular, with shaped sides
Offset litho printed
Made for Huntley & Palmers
H.15.2cm.   W.14.4cm.   D.8.6cm.

M.250-1983
'POMPEIAN' 1893
A casket
Offset litho printed
Made for Huntley & Palmers
H.16cm.   W.19cm.   D.9.4cm.

M.251-1983
'SHOWMAN' 1893
Triangular, with shaped sides
Offset litho printed
Made for Huntley & Palmers
H.16cm.   W.17.8cm.   D.12.6cm.

M.252-1983
'MAIL' 1893
With shaped ends
Offset litho printed
Made for Huntley & Palmers (for export)
H.5cm.   W.15.2cm.   D.9.5cm.

M.253-1983
'ALGERIAN' 1894
Quatrefoil-shaped
Offset litho printed
Made for Huntley & Palmers
H.9.3cm.   W.17.4cm.   D.16.6cm.

M.254-1983
'CAVALRY' 1894
Semi-circular, with shaped sides
Offset litho printed
Made for Huntley & Palmers
H.15.2cm.   W.14.4cm.   D.8.6cm.

M.255-1983
'ARABIAN NIGHTS' 1894
Semi-circular, with shaped sides
Offset litho printed
Made for Huntley & Palmers
H.15.2cm.   W.14.4cm.   D.8.6cm.

M.256-1983
'ITALIAN' 1894
Offset litho printed
Made for Huntley & Palmers
H.6.4cm.   W.16.4cm.   D.16.4cm.

M.257-1983
'INDIAN' 1894
A casket
Offset litho printed
Made for Huntley & Palmers
H.16cm.   W.19cm.   D.9.4cm.

M.258-1983
'MAY QUEEN' 1895
With curved sides
Offset litho printed
Made for Huntley & Palmers
H.5.6cm.   W.22cm.   D.8.7cm.

M.259-1983
'NAUTICAL' 1895
With shaped corners
Offset litho printed
Made by Huntley & Palmers
H.9.3cm.   W.16.5cm.   D.12.5cm.

M.260-1983
'MEXICAN' 1895
Quatrefoil-shaped
Offset litho printed
Made by Huntley & Palmers
H.9.3cm.   W.17.4cm.   D.16.6cm.

M.261-1983
'RECREATION' 1895
Offset litho printed
Made by Huntley & Palmers
H.6.4cm.   W.16.4cm.   D.16.4cm.

M.262-1983
'FLEMISH' 1895
With shaped ends
Offset litho printed
Made for Huntley & Palmers (for export)
H.5cm.   W.15.2cm.   D.9.5cm.

M.263-1983
'JAPANESE' 1895
Offset litho printed
Made for Huntley & Palmers (for export)
H.4.5cm   W.15.3cm.   D.9.6cm.

M.264-1983
'SCANDINAVIAN' 1896
Triangular, with shaped sides
Offset litho printed
Made for Huntley & Palmers
H.16cm.   W.17.8cm.   D.12.6cm.

M265-1983
'MIDSUMMER' 1896
Offset litho printed
Made for Huntley & Palmers
H.5.8cm.   W.24.5cm.   D.14.8cm.

M266-1983
'TOURNAMENT" 1896
Shaped oval
Offset litho printed
Made for Huntley & Palmers
H.15.3cm.   W.12.4cm.   D.11cm.

M.267-1983
'ANCIENT LOCK' 1896
A simulated wooden box with metal mounts and
lock ; with original liner inside
Offset litho printed with embossing
Made for Huntley & Palmers
H.4.5cm.   W.20.5cm.   D.15.3cm.

M.268-1983
'COASTGUARD' 1897
Shaped oval
Offset litho printed
Made for Huntley & Palmers
H.15.3cm.   W.12.4cm.   D.11cm.

M.269-1983
'ARCTIC' 1897
Shaped oval
Offset litho printed
Made for Huntley & Palmers
H.15.3cm.   W.12.4cm.   D.11cm.

M.270-1983
'SEVRES' 1897
A casket on feet
Offset litho printed
Made for Huntley & Palmers
H.16cm.   W.16cm.   D.13cm.

M.271-1983
'BASKET' 1897
A lidded basket with collapsible handle, and
clasp fastening
Offset litho printed with embossing
Made for Huntley & Palmers
H. (excluding handle) 11.5cm.   W.18.6cm.
D.14.3cm.

M.272-1983
'OLD TIMES' 1897
Offset litho printed
Made for Huntley & Palmers
H.5.8cm.   W.24.5cm.   D.14.8cm.

M.273-1983
'DELFT' 1897
Offset litho printed
Made for Huntley & Palmers
H.4.5cm.   W.20.5cm.   D.153cm.

M.274-1983
'HENLEY' 1898
Offset litho printed
Made for Huntley & Palmers
H.9.2cm.   W.13.5cm.   D.13.5cm.

M.275-1983
'SHAMROCK' 1898
Offset litho printed
Made for Huntley & Palmers
H.5.8cm.   W.24.5cm.   D.14.8cm.

M.276-1983
'MOROCCO' 1898
A simulated leather lidded basket with
collapsible handle and clasp fastening
Made for Huntley & Palmers
H. (excluding handle) 11.5cm.   W.18.6cm.
D.14.3cm.

M.277-1983
'SLEDGE' 1898
With scenes of Russian life
Offset litho printed
Made for Huntley & Palmers
H.4.5cm.   W.20.5cm.   D.15.3cm.

M.278-1983
'ORIENT' 1899
A simulated leather-bound suitcase
Offset litho printed with embossing
Made for Huntley & Palmers
H.4.5cm.   W.20.5cm.   D.15.3cm.

M.279-1983
'IVORY' 1899
A simulated carved ivory casket with handle,
with scenes from the life of Queen Elizabeth
Offset litho printed, with embossing
Made for Huntley & Palmers
H.8.5cm.   W.23cm.

M.280-1983
'MINIATURES' 1899
A vase on stand, with portraits on the four
faces and lid
Offset litho printed with embossing
Made for Huntley & Palmers
H.18.4cm.   W.16cm.   D.16cm.

M.281-1983
'VIENNESE' 1899
A simulated tooled leather basket, with
collapsible handle, and clasp fastening
Offset litho printed with embossing
Made for Huntley & Palmers
H. (excluding handle) 11.5cm.   W.18.6cm.
D.14.3cm.

M.282-1983
'AFRICAN' 1899
Offset litho printed with embossing
Made for Huntley & Palmers
H.9.2cm.   W.13.5cm.   D.13.5cm.

M.283-1983
'WITH DOG AND GUN' 1899
Offset litho printed with embossing
Made for Huntley & Palmers
H.9.2cm.   W.13.5cm.   D.13.5cm.

M.284-1983
'LIBRARY' 1900
Eight books bound by a strap
Offset litho printed
Made for Huntley & Palmers
H.16cm.   W.16cm.   D.12cm.

M.285-1983
'NAVY' 1900
Offset litho printed with embossing
Made for Huntley & Palmers
H.9.2cm.   W.13.5cm.   D.13.5cm.

M.286-1983
'FLORAL' 1900
A casket with handle
Offset litho printed
Made for Huntley & Palmers
H. (excluding handle) 8.6cm.   W.23cm.
D.12.5cm.

M.287-1983
'ARTIST' 1900
An artist's palette with three brushes attached,
and clasp fastening
Offset litho printed
Made for Huntley & Palmers
H.5cm.   W.24.6cm.   D.19.6cm.

M.288-1983
INDIAN c.1900
Offset litho printed
Made for Huntley & Palmers (for export)
H.5.3cm.   W.15cm.   D.9.2cm.

M289-1983
'MOSAIC' 1901
A casket with handle, with scenes of medieval
jousting
Offset litho printed with embossing
Made for Huntley & Palmers
H. (excluding handle) 8.6cm.   W.23cm.
D.12.5cm.

M.290-1983
'LITERATURE' 1901
Eight books with simulated tooled leather
bindings and marbled end papers, bound by a
strap
Offset litho printed with embossing
Made for Huntley & Palmers
H.16cm.   W.16cm.   D.12cm.

M.291-1983
'CANTEEN' 1901
A simulated straw satchel, with cardboard
handle and patent clasp
Offset litho printed with embossing
Made for Huntley & Palmers
H.7cm.   W.17.7cm.   D.15.2cm.

M.292-1983
'GAINSBOROUGH' 1902
An artist's palette with three brushes attached
and clasp fastening, with a reproduction of
Gainsborough's portrait of the Duchess of
Devonshire
Offset litho printed
Made for Huntley & Palmers
H.5cm.   W.24.6cm.   D.19.6cm.

M.293-1983
'ARCADIAN' 1902
A casket with handle, on ball feet
Offset litho printed
Made for Huntley & Palmers
H. (excluding handle) 14.6cm.   W.16.5cm.
D.15.5cm.

M.294-1983
'HUNTSMAN' 1902
The lid in the form of a framed picture
Offset litho printed
Made for Huntley & Palmers
H.5cm.   W.34.5cm.   D.21.8cm.

M.295-1983
'LOG' 1902
A satchel with patent clasp, decorated with
insects and lizards on a log
Offset litho printed with embossing
Made for Huntley & Palmers
H.7cm.   W.17.5cm.

M.296-1983
'CAIRO' 1902
A hexagonal Moorish table
Offset litho printed
Made for Huntley & Palmers
H.16.5cm.   W.16.2cm.

M.297-1983
'SYRIAN' 1903
A hexagonal Moorish table
Offset litho printed with embossing
Made for Huntley & Palmers
H.16.5cm.   W.16.2cm.

M.298-1983
'WATTEAU' 1903
A casket with handle, on ball feet
Offset litho printed
Made for Huntley & Palmers
H. (excluding handle) 14.6cm.   W.16.5cm.
D.15.5cm.

M.299-1983
'WAVERLEY' 1903
Eight books by Walter Scott with simulated
tooled leather bindings, bound with a strap
Offset litho printed with embossing
Made for Huntley & Palmers
H.16cm.   W.16cm.   D.12cm.

M.300-1983
'SUNSET' 1903
The lid in the form of a framed picture
Offset litho printed
Made for Huntley & Palmers
H.5cm.   W.34.5cm.   D.21.8cm.

M.301-1983
'WALLET' 1903
A simulated snakeskin satchel with handle and
patent clasp
Offset litho printed with embossing
Made for Huntley & Palmers
H.7cm.   W.17.7cm.   D.15.2cm.

M.302-1983
'JEWEL CASE' 1903
Simulating leather; recessed handle
Offset litho printed
Made for Huntley & Palmers
H.7cm.   W.16.8cm.   D.16.8cm.

M.303-1983
'HANDBAG' 1904
A simulated pigskin handbag
Offset litho printed
Made for Huntley & Palmers
H. (excluding handle) 16cm.   W.20.6cm.
D.9.7cm.

M.304-1983
'HAMPER' 1904
An upright simulated wicker basket with label
pull-tab
Offset litho printed with embossing
Made for Huntley & Palmers
H.16.4cm.   Diam.16.3cm.

M.305-1983
'BUHL' 1904
Simulating Boulle work; recessed handle
Offset litho printed
Made for Huntley & Palmers
H.7cm.   W.16.8cm.   D.16.8cm.

M.306-1983
'KASHMIR' 1904
A hexagonal Moorish table, with animals'
heads
Offset litho printed
Made for Huntley & Palmers
H.16.5cm.   W.16.2cm.

M.307-1983
'ENAMEL' 1904
A casket with handle, on ball feet
Offset litho printed with embossing
Made for Huntley & Palmers
H. (excluding handle) 14.6cm.   W.16.5cm.
D.15.5cm.

M.308-1983
Metal liner for Biscuit Tin: 'WORKBASKET'
1904
Direct printed (?)
Made for Huntley & Palmers
H.7cm.   W.16.5cm.   D.16.8cm.

M.309-1983
'BOOKSTAND' 1905
A simulated wooden bookstand on ball feet
Offset litho printed with embossing
Made for Huntley & Palmers
H.16cm.   W.12.7cm.   D.10.8cm.

M.310-1983
'MAHOGANY' 1905
Offset litho printed with embossing
Made for Huntley & Palmers
H. (excluding knob) 7cm.   W.15.8cm.
D.10.7cm.

M.311-1983
'OVAL BASKET' 1905
Metal liner inside an oval straw basket
Direct printed (?)
Made for Huntley & Palmers
(Basket) H.9cm.   W.18.5cm.   D.12.5cm.

M.312-1983
'CYPRUS' 1905
A casket on feet, with drop handles
Imitation oxidised copper, with embossing
Made for Huntley & Palmers
H.11.5cm.   W.19.5cm.   D.14.2cm.

M.313-1983
'RETICULE' 1905
A simulated leather handbag
Offset litho printed
Made for Huntley & Palmers
H. (excluding handle) 16cm.   W.20.6cm.
D.9.7cm.

M.314-1983
'CHERRIES' 1905
With clasp fastening
Offset litho printed with embossing
Made by Barringer, Wallis & Manners for
Huntley & Palmers
H.6cm.   W.17.5cm.   D.15.7cm.

M.315-1983
'PLATES' 1906
A stacked pile of Derby porcelain plates
Offset litho printed
Marked: Rd. No. 420706
Made by Hudson Scott & Sons for Huntley &
Palmers
H.6cm.   Diam.21.2cm.

M.316-1983
'MARQUETRY' 1906
Offset litho printed
Made for Huntley & Palmers
H.4cm.   W.16.5cm.   D.16.5cm.

M.317-1983
'GLOBE' 1906
A globe on four ball feet
Offset litho printed
Made for Huntley & Palmers
H.18cm. (including knob)

M.318-1983
'ITALIAN' 1906
Offset litho printed
Made for Huntley & Palmers (for export)
H.6.8cm.   W.18.1cm.   D.11.1cm.

M.319-1983
'APPLES' 1907
With clasp fastening
Offset litho printed with embossing
Made by Barringer, Wallis & Manners for
Huntley & Palmers
H.6cm.   W.17.5cm.   D.15.7cm.

M.320-1983
'IRON CHEST' 1907
An antique coffer
Offset litho printed with embossing
Marked: Regd. No. 460206
Made by Huntley, Boorne & Stevens for
Huntley & Palmers
H.9.2cm.   W.19cm.   D.10.9cm.

M.321-1983
'FIELD GLASS CASE' 1907
A simulated pig-skin leather binocular case
with collapsible handle
Offset litho printed
Marked: Rd. No. 462,687
Made by Huntley, Boorne & Stevens for
Huntley & Palmers
H. (excluding handle) 14.2cm.   W.17.7cm.
D.9.5cm.

M.322-1983
'CREEL' 1907
An angler's basket
Offset litho printed with embossing
Marked: Regd. No. 486204
Made by Huntley, Boorne & Stevens for
Huntley & Palmers
H.15cm.   W.19.5cm.   D.13.5cm.

M.323-1983
'DRAGON' 1907
Offset litho printed with embossing
Made for Huntley & Palmers
H.4.3cm.   W.16.5cm.   D.16.5cm.

M.324-1983
'BUHL' 1907
Oval, with recessed handle; simulating
Boulle work
Offset litho printed
Made by Huntley, Boorne & Stevens for
Huntley & Palmers (for export)
H.4.5cm.   W.18cm.   D.11.5cm.

M.325-1983
'NASTURTIUMS' 1908
Oval
Offset litho printed with embossing
Made for Huntley & Palmers
H.5.6cm.   W.21cm.   D.11.6cm.

M.326-1983
'SYLVAN VASE' 1908
A two-handled vase on stand
Offset litho printed with embossing
Made by Barringer, Wallis & Manners for
Huntley & Palmers
H. (excluding knob) 18cm.   Diam.14cm.

M.327-1983
'HARVEST' 1908
Hexagonal
Offset litho printed with embossing
Made for Huntley & Palmers
H.8.4cm.   W.19.5cm.

M.328-1983
'SATCHEL' 1908
An imitation snakeskin handbag
Offset litho printed with embossing
Marked: Rd. No. 493,911
Made by Huntley, Boorne & Stevens for
Huntley & Palmers
H. (excluding handle) 12cm.   W.19cm.

M.329-1983
'EMBROIDERY' 1908
A simulated embroidered cushion with curved
sides
Offset litho printed
Made for Huntley & Palmers
H.5.5cm.   W.22cm.   D.17cm.

M.330-1983
'STATIONERY CASE' 1908
A simulated tooled leather stationery box with
sloping lid and curved front
Offset litho printed
Marked: Regd No. 503,488
Made by Huntley, Boorne & Stevens for
Huntley & Palmers
H.16.9cm.   W.14cm.   D.14.7cm.

M.331-1983
'LUSITANIA' 1908
With a scene of the Cunard liner 'Lusitania'
arriving at New York on its maiden voyage
in 1907; shaped ends
Offset litho printed
Made by Huntley, Boorne & Stevens for
Huntley & Palmers
H.7cm.   W.24.4cm.   D.9.6cm.

M.332-1983
'CLOISONNE' 1908
Oval, with recessed handle
Offset litho printed
Made by Huntley, Boorne & Stevens for
Huntley & Palmers (for export)
H.4.5cm.   W.18cm.   D.11.5cm.

M.333-1983
'NUTS' 1908
A vase on four feet
Offset litho printed with embossing
Made by Barringer, Wallis & Manners for
Huntley & Palmers (for export)
H. (excluding knob) 15.5cm.   W.7.5cm.
D.7.5cm.

M.334-1983
'FLEMISH VASE' 1909
A vase with shaped sides
Offset litho printed with embossing
Made by Barringer, Wallis & Manners for
Huntley & Palmers
H. (excluding knob) 21.5cm.   W.15cm.
D.7cm.

M.335-1983
'ROSES' 1909
A mounted vase on three feet
Offset litho printed
Made for Huntley & Palmers
H. (excluding knob) 19cm.   W.20cm.

M.336-1983
'WATERLILIES' c.1909
A bowl on four feet
Offset litho printed
Made for Huntley & Palmers
H.15cm.   D.22cm.

M.337-1983
'SEVRES' 1909
A casket, with a pair of roll-top articulated
lids
Offset litho printed
Made for Huntley & Palmers
H.20cm.   W.22.6cm.   D.14.8cm.

M.338-1983
'MARBLE' 1909
A simulated marble pedestal with four
female statues in niches
Offset litho printed with embossing
Made by Huntley, Boorne & Stevens for
Huntley & Palmers
H.18.4cm.   W.12.6cm.   D.12.6cm.

M.339-1983
'DELFT' 1909
With shaped corners
Offset litho printed with embossing
Made for Huntley & Palmers
H.9.8cm.   W.18.5cm.   D.13.2cm.

M.340-1983
'BOOKS' 1909
Seven books between bookends
Offset litho printed
Marked: Regd. No. 526854
Made by Huntley, Boorne & Stevens for
Huntley & Palmers
H.10.1cm.   W.22.3cm.   D.10cm.

M.341-1983
'IRON CHEST A.Y.P.E.' 1909
An antique coffer
Offset litho printed with embossing
Marked: Regd. No. 460206
Made by Huntley, Boorne & Stevens for
Huntley & Palmers, for the Alaska, Yukon,
Pacific Exposition at Seattle, Washington
in 1909
H.9.2cm.   W.19cm.   D.10.9cm.

M.342-1983
'NANKIN' 1910
Simulating a Chinese jar on an ebonised
wood stand
Offset litho printed
Made for Huntley and Palmers
H.17.5cm.   Diam.11cm.

M.343-1983
'STATUARY' 1910
A simulated marble pedestal with four female
female statues in niches
Offset litho printed with embossing
Made by Huntley, Boorne & Stevens for
Huntley & Palmers
H.18.4cm.   W.12.6cm.   D.12.6cm.

M.344-1983
'COUNTRYSIDE' 1910
A vase with shaped sides
Offset litho printed with embossing
Made by Barringer, Wallis & Manners for
Huntley & Palmers
H. (excluding knob) 18cm.   W.17.4cm.
D.6.7cm.

M.345-1983
'VENICE' 1910
A two-handled bowl on four feet
Offset litho printed with embossing
Made for Huntley & Palmers
H.17cm.   Diam.22cm.

M.346-1983
'RUSTIC' 1910
A casket of simulated logs
Offset litho printed
Made for Huntley & Palmers
H.11cm.   W.18cm.   D.9.8cm.

M.347-1983
'SENTRY BOX' 1910
A sentry box
Offset litho printed with embossing
Marked: Reg. No. 522207
Made by Huntley, Boorne & Stevens for
Huntley & Palmers (for export)
H.18cm.   W.6.5cm.   D.6.5cm.

M.348-1983
'STORIES' 1910
A handled satchel containing three books
Offset litho printed
Made for Huntley & Palmers (for export)
H.10cm.   W.10.5cm.   D.6.1cm.

M.349-1983
'DICKENS' 1911
Eight books by Charles Dickens, with
simulated tool leather bindings, held by a
strap
Offset litho printed with embossing
Made for Huntley & Palmers
H.16cm.   W.16cm.   D.12cm.

M.350-1983
'LANTERN' 1911
A lantern with conical lid, and ring
Offset litho printed with embossing
Marked: Regd. No. 548328
Made by Huntley, Boorne & Stevens for
Huntley & Palmers
H.23cm.   Diam. of base 13cm.

M.351-1983
'CABINET' 1911
A glazed china cabinet
Offset litho printed with embossing
Marked: Regd. No. 558142
Made by Huntley, Boorne & Stevens for
Huntley & Palmers
H.18.4cm.   W.14.5cm.   D.8.5cm.

M.352-1983
'CAMEO' 1911
A casket on feet
Offset litho printed
Made for Huntley & Palmers
H.12.5cm.   W.20cm.   D.14.2cm.

M.353-1983
'CAUCASIAN' 1911
A casket on feet
Offset litho printed with embossing
Made for Huntley & Palmers
H.13.2cm.   W.20.2cm.   D.14cm.

M.354-1983
'WESTWARD HO' 1911
A hexagonal vase on stand
Offset litho printed
Made for Huntley & Palmers
H. (excluding knob) 20.5cm.   W.12.5cm.

M.355-1983
'TOKYO' 1911
Offset litho printed with embossing
Made by Huntley, Boorne & Stevens for
Huntley & Palmers
H.8cm.   W.16.8cm.   D.10.2cm.

M.356-1983
'TOBY JUG' 1911
A Toby Jug
Offset litho printed with embossing
Marked: Rd. 569652
Made by Hudson Scott & Sons for Huntley &
Palmers
H.16cm.   Diam.12.7cm.

M.357-1983
'CARNIVAL' 1911
A Japanese paper lantern
Offset litho printed
Marked: Rgd. No. 556543
Made by Huntley, Boorne & Stevens for
Huntley & Palmers
H.12.3cm.   Diam.8cm.

M.358-1983
'SHELL' 1912
A shell-shaped casket on four feet
Offset litho printed with embossing
Marked: Rd. 574980
Made for Huntley & Palmers
H.10cm.   W.18.9cm.   D.18.9cm.

M.359-1983
'BELL' 1912
A bell
Imitation oxidized copper, with embossing
Made for Huntley & Palmers
H. (excluding handle) 15.5cm.   Diam.15.7cm.

M.360-1983
'CHIVALRY' 1912
A casket
Imitation oxidized silver with embossing
Made for Huntley & Palmers
H.12.5cm.   W.28.3cm.   D.13.3cm.

M.361-1983
'WORCESTER VASE' 1912
A jar
Offset litho printed
Marked: Regd. No. 385,995
Made by Barringer, Wallis & Manners for
Huntley & Palmers
H.22.5cm.   W.11cm.   D.11cm.

M.362-1983
'POPPIES' 1912
Offset litho printed with embossing
Made for Huntley & Palmers
H.6cm.   W.16.6cm.   D.16.6cm.

M.363-1983
'PENCIL BOX' 1912
A simulated straped leather case with handle
Offset litho printed with embossing
Made for Huntley & Palmers
H. (excluding handle) 5.5cm.   W.20.6cm.
D.5.7cm.

M.364-1983
'LOCKET' 1912
Oval, with hook and clasp
Offset litho printed
Marked: Redgd. No. 592589
Made by Huntley, Boorne & Stevens for
Huntley & Palmers
H.4.5cm.   W.18cm.   D.11.5cm.

M.365-1983
'CAMERA' 1913
A Box Brownie Camera, with collapsible
handle
Offset litho printed with embossing
Marked: Rd. 610604
Made by Hudson Scott & Sons for Huntley &
Palmers
H. (excluding handle) 10cm.   W.10.3cm.
D.5.8cm.

M.366-1983
'GLOVE BOX' 1913
With a scene of a carriage on the foldover lid
Offset litho printed with embossing
Made for Huntley & Palmers
H.5.7cm.   W.27.7cm.   D.9.3cm.

M.367-1983
'KING WENCESLAS' 1913
An open book
Offset litho printed
Marked: Rd.,598833   Rd. 608869
Made by Hudson Scott & Sons for Huntley &
Palmers
H.4.7cm.   W.27cm.   D.16.2cm.

M.368-1983
'SCREEN' 1913
A 4-fold screen with Japanesse decoration
Offset litho printed with embossing
Marked: Regd. No. 611071
Made by Huntley, Boorne & Stevens for
Huntley & Palmers
H.19cm.   W.17cm.   D.12.3cm.

M.369-1983
'PEACOCK CASKET' 1913
A casket on feet
Offset litho printed with embossing
Made for Huntley & Palmers
H.13cm.   W.18.2cm.   D.18.2cm.

M.370-1983
'SUNDIAL' 1913
A sundial with collapsible pointer
Offset litho printed with embossing
Marked: Regd. No. 560319
Made by Huntley, Boorne & Stevens for
Huntley & Palmers
H. (excluding pointer) 20cm.   W.13cm.
D.13cm.

M.371-1983
'EAST AND WEST' 1913
A two-handled vase with shaped sides
Offset litho printed with embossing
Made by Barringer, Wallis & Manners for
Huntley & Palmers
H. (excluding knob) 25.3cm.   W.21.6cm.
D.7.7cm.

M.372-1983
'SILHOUETTE' 1914
Triangular, on feet
Offset litho printed
Marked: Rd. No. 619012
Made for Huntley & Palmers
H.18.5cm.   W.12.6cm.

M.373-1983
'EASEL' 1914
An easel with framed reproductions of
J. B. Greuze's paintings *The Milkmaid* and
Boy with a Rabbit
Offset litho printed
Made for Huntley & Palmers
H.21cm.   W.14cm.   D.10cm.

M.374-1983
'MIRROR' 1914
The lid to be used as a hand mirror
Offset litho printed with embossed lid
Made by Barringer, Wallis & Manners for
Huntley & Palmers

M.375-1983
'MIRROR' 1914
The lid to be used as a hand mirror
Offset litho printed with embossed lid
Made by Barringer, Wallis & Manners for
Huntley & Palmers
H.7.5cm.   W.16.5cm.   D.10.1cm.

M.376-1983
'CANNON' 1914
A wheeled cannon, with two pictures of
H.M.S. Victory
Offset litho printed
Made for Huntley & Palmers
H.12cm.   W.13cm.   D.6.4cm.

M.377-1983
'SENTRIES' 1914
A sentry box
Offset litho printed with embossing
Marked: Regd. No. 643116
Made by Huntley, Boorne & Stevens for
Huntley & Palmers
H.18cm.   W.6.5cm.   D.6.5cm.

M.378-1983
'TORTOISESHELL CASKET' 1914
A casket on ball feet
Offset litho printed with embossing
Made for Huntley & Palmers
H.12.5cm.   W.22.8cm.   D.15cm.

M.379-1983
'PHEASANT' 1914
Offset litho printed with embossing
Made for Huntley & Palmers
H.8.7cm.   W.20.8cm.   D.17cm.

M.380-1983
'WALLET' 1914
An imitation pigskin handbag with string
handles
Offset litho printed (red)
Made by Barringer, Wallis & Manners for
Huntley & Palmers
H.12.5cm.   W.14cm.   D.5.2cm.

M.381-1983
'WALLET' 1914
An imitation pigskin handbag with string
handles
Offset litho printed (brown)
Made by Barringer, Wallis & Manners for
Huntley & Palmers
H.12.5cm.   W.14cm.   D.5.2cm.

M.382-1983
'WALLET' 1914
An imitation pigskin handbag with string
handles
Offset litho printed (blue)
Made by Barringer, Wallis & Manners for
Huntley & Palmers
H.12.5cm.   W.14cm.   D.5.2cm.

M.383-1983
'WATER BOTTLE' 1915
A circular military water bottle
Offset litho printed with embossing
Made for Huntley & Palmers
H.16cm.   W.12.8cm.   D.4.2cm.

M.384-1983
'INDIAN' 1920
A casket issued to commemorate the Prince of
Wales' visit to India
Offset litho printed
Made by Barringer, Wallis & Manners for
Huntley & Palmers
H.6.5cm.   W15cm.

M.385-1983
'TAPESTRY' 1920
With a reproduction of Sir T. Lawrence's
painting *Master Lambton* on the lid; clasp
fastening
Offset litho printed
Made by Barringer, Wallis & Manners for
Huntley & Palmers
H.5.7cm.   W.21.7cm.   D.17.5cm.

M.386-1983
'CHINESE JAR' 1920
A two-handled Chinese jar
Offset litho printed with embossing
Made by Barringer, Wallis & Manners for
Huntley & Palmers
H.22.5cm.   W.18cm.   D.9.5cm.

M.387-1983
'PENNY IN THE SLOT MACHINE'
1923
A biscuit-dispensing machine and money box
Offset litho printed
Made for Huntley & Palmers
H.22.5cm.   W.14cm.   D.9cm.

M.388-1983
'WINDMILL' 1924
A windmill
Offset litho printed
Made for Huntley & Palmers
H.23.5cm.   W.9.3cm.   D.9.3cm.
(excluding blades)

M.389 and a-1983
'EGYPTIAN VASES' 1924
A pair of vases with drop handles
Offset litho printed with embossing
Made for Huntley & Palmers
H.22.5cm.   Diam.10cm.

M.390-1983
'BOOK' 1924
A book (brown)
Offset litho printed
Made by Huntley, Boorne & Stevens for
Huntley & Palmers
H.3.5cm.   W.24.9cm.   D.18cm.

M.391-1983
'WEMBLEY' 1924
Made for sale at the British Empire
Exhibition, Wembley, 1924
Made for Huntley & Palmers
H.4cm.   W.16.8cm.   D.10.4cm.

M.392-1983
'LACQUER' 1925
Offset litho printed
Made for Huntley & Palmers
H.5.5cm.   W.15.6cm.   D.15.6cm.

M.393-1983
'BISCUIT BOX' 1925
Aluminium, with embossing
Marked: Pat.26744/24
Made by N. C. Joseph for Huntley & Palmers
H.13cm.   Diam.10.5cm.

M.394-1983
'MAPLEWOOD CASKET' 1926
With shaped corners; simulating inlaid wood
Offset litho printed
Marked:No.4813
Made for Huntley & Palmers
H.7.3cm.   W.23.5cm.   D.14.5cm.

M.395-1983
'HOLIDAY HAUNTS' 1926
A vase
Offset litho printed
Manufacturers mark: H B & S L
Made by Huntley, Boorne & Stevens for
Huntley & Palmers
H.19.5cm.   W.8.5cm.   D.7.7cm.

M.396-1983
'FRUIT BASKET' 1926
A handled basket filled with fruit
Offset litho printed with embossed lid
Made for Huntley & Palmers
H. (excluding handle) 12.7cm   W.12.9cm.
D.8.5cm.

M.397-1983
'KITCHEN RANGE' 1926
A kitchen range with two opening doors
Offset litho printed with embossing
Manufacturers mark: H. B. & S. Ltd. R.
Made by Huntley, Boorne & Stevens for
Huntley & Palmers
H.8.7cm.   W.13.7cm.   D.5.3cm.

M.398-1983
'F.A. CUP' 1926
The Football Association Cup
Aluminium with embossing
Made by N. C. Joseph Ltd. for Huntley &
Palmers in preparation for Reading Football
Club's anticipated victory at Wembley in 1927.
The Club lost in the Semi-final, and this
biscuit tin was never issued in Great Britain
H.21cm.   Diam. of base 9.5cm.

M.399-1983
Display Item: 'F.A. CUP' 1926
The Football Association Cup
Aluminium with embossing
Made by N. C. Joseph Ltd. for Huntley &
Palmers for display purposes (see entry for
M.398-1983)
H.40cm.   Diam. of base 21cm.

M.400-1983
'MORLAND CASKET' 1927
Simulating wood; with a reproduction of a
painting by G. Morland on the lid
Offset litho printed with embossing
Made for Huntley & Palmers
H.3.7cm.   W.25.7cm.   D.20.8cm.

M.401-1983
'TANK' 1927
An army tank
Offset litho printed
Made for Huntley & Palmers
H.8.5cm.   W.18.7cm.   D.8cm.

M.402-1983
'SANDALWOOD CASKET' 1927
Copied from a carved sandalwood casket
presented to Lord and Lady Palmer during a
world tour in 1926
With its original packing instructions and
advertisement
Offset litho printed with embossing
Made by Barringer, Wallis & Manners for
Huntley & Palmers (for export)
H.10.5cm.   W.25.5cm.   D.18cm.

M.403-1983
'INKSTAND' 1928
A cylindrical pen tray on stand, containing its
original ceramic inkwell; hunting scenes on
the lid
Offset litho printed
Made by Huntley, Boorne & Stevens for
Huntley & Palmers
H.6.5cm.   W.23.7cm.   D.6.9cm.

M.404 and a-1983
'CHINESE VASE' 1928
A pair of octagonal vases
Offset litho printed
Made by Huntley, Boorne & Stevens for
Huntley & Palmers
H.26cm.   W. of base 6.5cm.

M.405-1983
'EGGSTAND' 1928
An egg stand with three detachable egg cups
Aluminium
Marked: Pat 26744/24
Made by N. C. Joseph Ltd. for Huntley &
Palmers
H.15cm. (including handle)   Diam.11.5cm.
(at base)

M.406-1983
'GRANDFATHER CLOCK' 1929
A simulated lacquer chinoiserie grandfather
clock
Offset litho printed
Marked: No. 10721
Made for Huntley & Palmers
H.29.3cm.   W.9.9cm.   D.6.7cm.

M.407-1983
'ITALIAN CASKET' 1929
A casket on feet
Offset litho printed
Made for Huntley & Palmers
H.10cm.   W22.7cm.   D15.3cm.

M.408-1983
'PERAMBULATOR' 1930
A pram with a child inside
Offset litho printed
Marked: No. 12701
Made by Barringer, Wallis & Manners for
Huntley & Palmers
H.12cm.   W.20cm.   D.8.3cm.

M.409-1983
'NEEDLEWORK' 1930
A hexagonal simulated straw basket
Offset litho printed
Made for Huntley & Palmers
H.3.7cm.   W.15.2cm.

M.410-1983
'BOOK' 1930
In imitation of the book Het Boek Der Gebeden,
1704, in the British Museum
Made by Huntley, Boorne & Stevens for
Huntley & Palmers
H.3.5cm.   W.24.9cm.   D.18cm.

M.411-1983
'FARMHOUSE' 1931
A farmhouse with an attached fence
Offset litho printed
Manufacturers mark: H. B. & S. Ltd. Reading
Made by Huntley, Boorne & Stevens for
Huntley & Palmers
H.10.5cm.   W.15.5cm.   D.16.2cm. (with
fence extended)

M.412-1983
'GLOVE BOX' 1931
Copied from an Indian inlaid wooden box on
ball feet which is in Metal Box Co archives,
Mansfield
Offset litho printed
Made by Barringer, Wallis & Manners for
Huntley & Palmers
H.5.3cm.   W.29.2cm.   D.11.5cm.

M.413-1983
'WOOD AND IVORY BOX' 1931
In its original cardboard box
Offset litho printed with embossing
Manufacturers mark: H. B. & S. Ltd. Reading,
Made by Huntley, Boorne & Stevens for
Huntley & Palmers
H.4.2cm.   W.12cm.   D.8.4cm.

M.414-1983
'CHOCOLATE RIVIERA' 1931
Offset litho printed
Manufacturers mark: H. B. & S. Ltd. Reading
Made by Huntley, Boorne & Stevens for
Huntley & Palmers
H.5cm.   W.21.5cm.   D.16cm.

M.415-1983
'MONEY BOX' 1933
A money box in the form of a pillar box
Offset litho printed
Made by Huntley, Boorne & Stevens for
Huntley & Palmers
H.13.5cm.   Diam.6.5cm.

M.416-1983
'VERONA' 1933
With one curved side, and a reproduction of
W. Holman Hunt's painting Valentine
rescuing Sylvia from Proteus on the lid
Offset litho printed
Manufacturers mark: H. B. & S. Ltd. Reading
Made by Huntley Boorne & Stevens for
Huntley & Palmers
H.4.5cm.   W.23.2cm.   D.17.5cm.

M.417-1983
'KING CHARLES' 1933
Curved sides; with a reproduction of
Frederick Goodall's painting The Happier
Days of Charles I on the lid
Offset litho printed
Made for Huntley & Palmers
H.4.7cm.   W.22cm.   D.18cm.

M.418-1983
'JOHN GINGER' 1933
Triangular
Offset litho printed
Made for Huntley & Palmers
H.13.5cm.   W.11.7cm.

M.419 and a-1983
'WORCESTER VASES' 1934
A pair of octagonal vases
Offset litho printed
Made by Huntley, Boorne & Stevens for
Huntley & Palmers
H.26cm.   W. of base 6.5cm.

M.420-1983
'RIVOLI' 1934
With a reproduction of Jules Girardet's
painting A Difficult Passage on the lid
Offset litho printed
Made for Huntley & Palmers
H.7cm.   W.18cm.   D.9.7cm.

M.421-1983
'VILLAGE SHOP' 1935
With curved ends
Offset litho printed
Manufacturers mark: H. B. & S. Ltd. Reading
Made by Huntley, Boorne & Stevens for
Huntley & Palmers
H.4.7cm.   W.30.7cm.   D.14.9cm.

M.422-1983
'VAN TROMP' 1935
With a reproduction of J. Seymour Lucas'
painting A Whip for Van Tromp on the lid
Offset litho printed
Manufacturers mark: H. B. & S. Ltd. Reading
Made by Huntley, Boorne & Stevens for
Huntley & Palmers
H.7cm.   W.21.2cm.   D.14.8cm.

M.423-1983
'LOST CAUSE' 1935
With a reproduction of A. C. Gow's painting
A Lost Cause on the lid
Offset litho printed
Manufacturers mark: H. B. & S. Ltd. Reading
Made by Huntley, Boorne & Stevens for
Huntley & Palmers
H.7cm.   W.18cm.   D.9.7cm.

M.424-1983
'COCKTAIL TIME' 1935
With handle, and lid in two sections
Offset litho printed with embossing
Manufacturers mark: H. B. & S. Ltd. Reading
Made by Huntley, Boorne & Stevens for
Huntley & Palmers
H.5cm. W.21cm. D.10.5cm.

M.425-1983
'DUNKELD' 1935
Offset litho printed
Manufacturers mark: H. B. & S. Ltd.
Made by Huntley, Boorne & Stevens for
Huntley & Palmers
H.4.5cm. Diam.19.2cm.

M.426-1983
'HYACINTH' 1935
Offset litho printed
Made for Huntley & Palmers
H.4.5cm. W.21cm. D.14.7cm.

M.427-1983
'SILVER JUBILEE' 1935
With portraits of George V and Queen Mary
on the lid
Offset litho printed
Made by Huntley, Boorne & Stevens for
Huntley & Palmers
H.10.6cm. Diam.12.9cm.

M.428-1983
'JAPANESE TEA CADDY' 1936
With shaped corners
Offset litho printed
Made by Barringer, Wallis & Manners for
Huntley & Palmers
H.17.8cm. W.11.9cm. D.8.5cm.

M.429-1983
'PENNY IN THE SLOT' 1936
A biscuit-dispensing machine with money-
box, decorated with elfs etc.
Offset litho printed
Made by Huntley, Boorne & Stevens for
Huntley & Palmers
H.23cm. W.11.6cm. D.9.6cm.

M.430-1983
'ROCKET' 1936
With curved ends, and a scene of
Stephenson's 'Rocket' on the lid
Offset litho printed
Manufacturer's mark: H. B. & S. Ltd.
Reading
Made by Huntley, Boorne & Stevenson for
Huntley & Palmers
H.4.7cm. W.30.7cm. D.14.9cm.

M.431-1983
'SPANISH' 1936
Offset litho printed
Made for Huntley & Palmers
H.4.5cm. W.21cm. D.14.7cm.

M.432-1983
'BONXIE' 1936
With a reproduction of J. C. Hook's painting
The Bonxie Shetland on the lid
Offset litho printed
Manufacturer's mark: H. B. & S. Ltd.
Reading
Made by Huntley, Boorne & Stevens for
Huntley & Palmers
H.7cm. W.18cm. D.9.7cm.

M.433-1983
'CORONATION' 1937
With portraits of George VI and Queen
Elizabeth on the lid
Offset litho printed
Manufacturer's mark: H. B. & S. Ltd.
Reading
Made by Huntley, Boorne & Stevens for
Huntley & Palmer
H.10.6cm. Diam.12.9cm.

M.434-1983
'JOHN O'GROATS' 1937
Offset litho printed
Made by Huntley, Boorne & Stevens for
Huntley & Palmers
H.10.6cm. Diam.12.9cm.

M.435-1983
'BISCUIT BARREL' 1937
Offset litho printed, with plastic knob
Made by Barringer, Wallis & Manners for
Huntley & Palmers
H.17cm. Diam. of base 10cm.

M.436-1983
'QUEEN ELIZABETH' 1937
Oval, with fluted sides
Offset litho printed
Made for Huntley & Palmers
H.7cm. W.24.2cm. D.19cm.

M.437-1983
'ZODIAC' 1937
Offset litho printed
Manufacturer's mark: H. B. & S. Ltd.
Reading
Made by Huntley, Boorne & Stevens for
Huntley & Palmers
H.5cm. W.21.7cm. D.14.5cm.

M.438-1983
'TWO STRINGS' 1938
With a reproduction of J. Pettie's painting
Two Strings to Her Bow on the lid
Offset litho printed
Made for Huntley & Palmers
H.8.5cm. Diam.18cm.

M.439-1983
'EVERYDAY TIN' 1938
Offset litho printed
Made for Huntley & Palmers
H.8.5cm. W.23.9cm. D.9.3cm.

M.440-1983
'BEDSIDE' 1938
Offset litho printed
Made for Huntley & Palmers
H.12cm. W.14.4cm. D.10cm.

M.441-1983
'VASE' 1938
A two-handled vase, with scenes of boats
Offset litho printed, with plastic knob
Manufacturer's mark: H. B. & S. Ltd.
Reading
Made by Huntley, Boorne & Stevens for
Huntley & Palmers
H.23cm. Diam. of base 7.3cm.

M.442-1983
'LEGEND' 1938
Offset litho printed with embossing
Made for Huntley & Palmers
H.6.7cm. W.16.9cm. D.15.4cm.

M.443-1983
'DALMATIAN' 1939
With shaped corners
Offset litho printed
Made by Barringer, Wallis & Manners for
Huntley & Palmers
H.6cm. W.26.8cm. D.9.9cm.

M.444-1983
'MUSES' 1939
With shaped corners; imitating wood
painted with Neo-classical decoration
Offset litho printed with embossing
Made for Huntley & Palmers
H.9.5cm. W.10.3cm. D.10.3cm.

M.445-1983
'BRASS PLAQUE' 1939
Offset litho printed; the brass lid with a hook
for hanging on the wall
Made for Huntley & Palmers
H.5.5cm. Diam.19.2cm.

W. & R. JACOB & CO.

M.446-1983
'ALICE' 1892
With scenes based on John Tenniel's
illustrations to Lewis Carroll's Through the
Looking Glass and What Alice found there
Offset litho printed
Made by Barringer, Wallis & Manners for
W. & R. Jacob & Co.
H.13cm. W.12.7cm. D.9.5cm.

M.447-1983
'COLUMBUS' 1892
Diamond-shaped; issued in celebration of the
400th anniversary of the discovery of America
by Christopher Columbus
Transfer-printed
Manufacturer's mark: Hudson Scott & Sons,
Carlisle
Made by Hudson Scott & Sons for
W. & R. Jacob & Co.
H.14cm. W.15cm. D.12cm.

M.448-1983
'BUTTERFLY' 1894
Offset litho printed
Made for W. & R. Jacob & Co.
H.6.5cm. W.22.5cm. D.15.5cm.

M.449-1983
'DRESDEN' 1896
Semi circular, with shaped sides
Transfer-printed with embossing
Manufacturer's mark: Hudson Scott & Sons,
Carlisle
Made by Hudson Scott & Sons for
W. & R. Jacob & Co.
H.13.5cm. W.14cm. D.10cm.

M.450-1983
'MANX' 1896
With shaped ends and scenes in the Isle of
Man
Transfer-printed with embossing
Manufacturer's mark: Hudson Scott & Sons
Carlisle
Made by Hudson Scott & Sons for
W. & R. Jacob & Co.
H.10.5cm. W.16.5cm. D10.3cm.

M.451-1983
'TORTOISESHELL' 1897
With shaped sides
Transfer-printed with embossing
Manufacturer's mark: Hudson Scott & Sons,
Carlisle
Made by Hudson Scott & Sons for
W. & R. Jacob & Co.
H.13.5cm. W.14cm. D.10cm.

M.452-1983
'SILVER POPPY' 1897
Transfer-printed
Made for W. & R. Jacob & Co.
H.6cm. W.18.5cm. D.18.5cm.

M.453-1983
'BASKET' 1898
A circular straw basket with collapsible
handle
Offset litho printed with embossing
Made for W. & R. Jacob & Co.
H.9.2cm. (excluding handle) Diam.16cm.

M.454-1983
'JEWEL CASKET' 1898
A simulated wooden chest
Offset litho printed
Made for W. & R. Jacob & Co.
H.8.7cm. W.19.3cm. D.10cm.

M.455-1983
'STATIONERY CASE' 1901
A stationery case, with inner partition and
sloping lid
Offset litho printed with embossing
Marked: Rd. No. 360519
Made by H. Bayerthall for
W. & R. Jacob & Co.
H.14.5cm. W.21cm. D.8.5cm.

M.456-1983
'WORCESTER BISCUIT JAR' 1901
A handled jar
Offset litho printed with embossing, and
glazed pottery knob
Marked: Rd. No. 33465 No. 337816
Made by H. Bayerthall for
W. & R. Jacob & Co.
H.14cm. (excluding handle and knob)
Diam.14.3cm.

M.457-1983
'CHRYSANTHEMUM BOX' 1901
Offset litho printed with embossing
Made for W. & R. Jacob & Co.
H.6cm. W.26cm. D.11.2cm.

M.458-1983
'GREAT EXPECTATIONS' 1902
With scenes of dogs on the lid
Offset litho printed with embossing, and
wool string handles
Made for W. & R. Jacob & Co.
H.7cm. W.11.4cm. D.9.9cm.

M.459-1983
'KITTENS' 1903
Offset litho printed, with wool string handles
Made for W. & R. Jacob & Co.
H.7cm. W.11.4cm. D.9.9cm.

M.460-1983
'BAGATELLE' 1904
A pinball machine
Offset litho printed
Made for W. & R. Jacob & Co. by
H. Bayerthall.
H.4.2cm.   W.28.2cm.   D.16.3cm.

M.461-1983
'COMPANIONS' 1905
With scenes of animals
Offset litho printed
Made for W. & R. Jacob & Co.
H.7.7cm.   W.11.3cm.   D.10cm.

M.462-1983
'SEE-SAW' 1906
Offset litho printed
Marked: Copyright
Made for W. & R. Jacob & Co.
H.5cm.   W.19.7cm.   D.7.4cm.

M.463-1983
'RUSSIAN CASKET' c.1912
A casket of simulated malacite; with a scene
of the Kremlin on the lid
Offset litho printed with embossing
Manufacturer's mark: B. W. & M. Ltd.
Mansfield No. 545
Made by Barringer, Wallis & Manners for
W. & R. Jacob & Co.
H.12.3cm.   W.18cm.   D.11.5cm.

M.464-1983
'BEACH PAIL' c.1922
A bucket with handle, with seaside scenes
(lid missing)
Offset litho printed
Marked: Pats. 178742 & 208369
Made by E. T. Gee for W. & R. Jacob & Co.
H.11.6cm. (excluding handle)   Diam.12cm.

M.465-1983
'HOUSEBOAT' 1923
A houseboat
Offset litho printed with embossing
Made by Hudson Scott & Sons for
W. & R. Jacob & Co.
H.11cm.   W.26.2cm.   D.12cm.

M.466-1983
'TEA CADDY' 1924
A Chinese lacquer cabinet
Offset litho printed with embossing
Manufacturer's mark: E. T. Gee & Sons Ltd.
Liverpool
Made by E. T. Gee for W. & R. Jacob & Co.
H.14cm.   W.17cm.   D.10cm.

M.467-1983
'VAN DYCK' 1925
A casket on feet; with a reproduction of
Van Dyck's portrait of Albert de Ligne,
Prince of Barbancon and Avenberg (wrongly
identified inside the lid as a self portrait by
Van Dyck)
Offset litho printed with embossing
Marked: No. 2200
Made by Barringer, Wallis & Manners for
W. & R. Jacob & Co.
H.7.6cm.   W.21.5cm.   D.14.5cm.

M.468-1983
'ELYSIAN' 1925
With shaped corners
Offset litho printed
Made for W. & R. Jacob & Co.
H.6.3cm.   W.18cm.   D.15.5cm.

M.469-1983
'ORIENT JAR' c.1926
A jar on three feet
Offset litho printed with embossing on lid
Marked: Regd.
Made by Barringer, Wallis & Manners for
W. & R. Jacob & Co.
H.15.2cm.   Diam.13.5cm.

M.470-1983
'BRISTOL CHINA CASKET' 1927
A casket on feet, with drop handles
Offset litho printed
Made for W. & R. Jacob & Co.
H.7cm.   W.21.3cm.   D.8.2cm.

M.471-1983
'TEA CADDY' 1927
A caddy on feet with handle, and scenes of
birds
Offset litho printed with embossing
Made by Hudson Scott & Sons for
W. & R. Jacob & Co.
H.16.5cm.   W.11.6cm.   D.11.6cm.

M.472-1983
'HUMMING TOP' 1928
A spinning top
Offset litho printed
Made by Hudson Scott & Sons for
W. & R. Jacob & Co.
H.22cm.   Diam.12.5cm.

M.473-1983
'TEA CADDY' 1928
A simulated red lacquer Japanese vase
Offset litho printed with embossing
Made for W. & R. Jacob & Co.
H.20.5cm.   W.13cm.   D.9cm.

M.474-1983
'LUCKY WHEEL' 1929
A mechanical fortune-telling money-box
Offset litho printed
Marked: No. 11896
Made by Barringer, Wallis & Manners for
W. & R. Jacob & Co.
H.19.8cm.   W.10.9cm.   D.7cm.

M.475-1983
'JACOBEAN LOG BOX' 1929
A simulated wooden casket on feet; the
sloping brass lid with a reproduction of a
painting by George Morland
Offset litho printed with embossing
Made by Barringer, Wallis & Manners for
W. & R. Jacob & Co.
H.11cm.   W.18cm.   D.9.5cm.

M.476-1983
'FLORAL TEA CADDY' 1930
Offset litho printed
Made for W. & R. Jacob & Co.
H.17.5cm.   W.13cm.   D.7.7cm.

M.477-1983
'CONCERTINA' 1930
A hexagonal playing musical accordion
Offset litho printed with leather handles
Manufacturer's mark: Hudson Scott & Sons
Ltd. Carlisle Eng.
Made by Hudson Scott & Sons for
W. & R. Jacob & Co.
H.13.2cm.   W.11cm.

M.478-1983
Cake Tin: 'CHRISTMAS CAKE FOR
CHILDREN' 1930
Octagonal; with scenes from Peter Pan
Offset litho printed
Made for W. & R. Jacob & Co.
H.6cm.   W.9.8cm.

M.479-1983
Cake Tin: 'CHRISTMAS CAKE FOR
CHILDREN' c.1931
Offset litho printed
Marked: 1370
Made for W. & R. Jacob & Co.
H.5.2cm.   Diam.9.6cm.

M.480-1983
Cake Tin: 'CHRISTMAS CAKE FOR
CHILDREN' 1932
Octagonal; with scenes of wild animals
Offset litho printed
Made for W. & R. Jacob & Co.
H.6cm.   W.9.8cm.

M.481-1983
'SHAGREEN' 1933
Simulating shagreen
Offset litho printed
Made by Barringer, Wallis & Manners for
W. & R. Jacob & Co.
H.8.4cm.   W.23.5cm.   D.8.6cm.

M.482-1983
Cake Tin: 'CHRISTMAS CAKE FOR
CHILDREN' 1934
Octagonal; with scenes of golliwogs
Made for W. & R. Jacob & Co.
H.6cm.   W.9.8cm.

M.483-1983
'TEA CADDY' 1935
With curved sides and reproductions after
J. L. David's paintings Madame Sériziat and
Monsieur Sériziat
Offset litho printed
Made by Hudson Scott & Sons for W. & R.
Jacob & Co.
H.15.5cm.   W.14cm.   D.9cm.

M.484-1983
'CORONATION COACH' 1936
A wheeled coach, in its original cardboard box
Offset litho printed
Made by Barringer, Wallis & Manners for
W. & R. Jacob & Co.
H.14cm.   W.23cm.   D.7.5cm.

M.485-1983
'MARJORIE' 1936
Shaped corners; with a reproduction of a
painting of a girl with a teddybear on the lid
Offset litho printed
Made for W. & R. Jacob & Co.
H.5cm.   W.23.2cm.   D.15.2cm.

M.486-1983
'DUTCH' 1936
With shaped corners
Offset litho printed
Made for W. & R. Jacob & Co.
H.4.3cm.   W.17.2cm.   D.11.5cm.

M.487-1983
Cake Tin: 'CHRISTMAS CAKE FOR
CHILDREN' 1936
With a scene of Father Christmas on the lid
Offset litho printed
Made for W. & R. Jacob & Co.
H.6.9cm.   Diam.11.7cm.

M.488-1983
'CARAVAN' 1937
A wheeled caravan with fold-away steps
Offset litho printed
Made by Barringer, Wallis & Manners for
W. & R. Jacob & Co.
H.13.5cm.   W.16cm.   D.7.5cm.

M.489-1983
'TEA CADDY' 1938
Shaped sides; simulating inlaid wood
Offset litho printed
Made for W. & R. Jacob & Co.
H.14cm.   D.17.5cm.   W.8.6cm.

M.490-1983
'BUTTERFLY' 1939
Offset litho printed with embossing
Made for W. & R. Jacob & Co.
H.8.5cm.   W.23.8cm.   D.9.3cm.

MACFARLANE, LANG & CO.

M.491-1983
'JUBILEE' 1887
With curved sides
Transfer-printed with embossing
Made for Macfarlane, Lang & Co.
H.16cm.   W.12.5cm.   D.9.5cm.

M.492-1983
'PIED PIPER OF HAMELIN' c.1893
Transfer-printed
Manufacturer's mark: Hudson Scott & Sons
Carlisle
Made by Hudson Scott & Sons for Macfarlane,
Lang & Co.
H.12cm.   W.14cm.   D.8.3cm.

M.493-1983
'VENETIAN' 1895
With shaped sides
Transfer printed with embossing
Made for Macfarlane, Lang & Co.
H.15cm.   W.14.4cm.   D.9.2cm.

M.494-1983
'GREATER BRITAIN' 1896
Commemorating Queen Victoria's Diamond
Jubilee, 1897; with curved sides
Transfer printed with embossing
Made for Macfarlane, Lang & Co.
H.16cm.   W.12.5cm.   D.9.5cm.

M.495-1983
'IVANHOE' 1896
With shaped sides
Transfer printed with embossing
Made for Macfarlane, Lang & Co.
H.15cm.   W.14.4cm.   D.9.2cm.

M.496-1983
'QUEEN BESS' 1896
With shaped sides
Offset litho printed with embossing
Made for Macfarlane, Lang & Co.
H.6.7cm. W.18.7cm. D.16.7cm.

M.497-1983
'VICAR OF WAKEFIELD' 1897
Pentagonal
Offset litho printed with embossing
Made for Macfarlane, Lang & Co.
H.11cm. W.17.7cm. D.12.4cm.

M.498-1983
'COURT' 1897
Offset litho printed with embossing
Made for Macfarlane, Lang & Co.
H.3.7cm. W.27.5cm. D.13.5cm.

M.499-1983
'CARRIAGE CLOCK' 1899
A simulated leather-cased carriage clock with a
calendar on one side, and recessed handle in
lid
Offset litho printed with incised decoration
Made for Macfarlane, Lang & Co.
H.15.7cm. W.11.9cm. D.8.2cm.

M.500-1983
'SHAKESPEAREAN' 1899
Offset litho printed with embossing
Made for Macfarlane, Lang & Co.
H.14cm. W.15cm. D.7.7cm.

M.501-1983
'NAVY' 1899
With curved sides
Offset litho printed
Made for Macfarlane, Lang & Co.
H.12.2cm. Diam.9cm.

M.502-1983
'MOROCCO CASKET' 1899
With shaped sides; simulating a Moroccan
leather casket
Offset litho printed with embossing
Made for Macfarlane, Lang & Co.
H.6.5cm. W.15cm. D.15cm.

M.503-1983
'POKERWORK' 1900
Simulating pokerwork
Offset litho printed with embossing
Made for Macfarlane, Lang & Co.
H.8cm. W.20.5cm. D.9.9cm.

M.504-1983
'MIRROR' 1900
Oval, with mirror in the lid
Offset litho printed
Made for Macfarlane, Lang & Co.
H.7.7cm. W.14cm. D.9.3cm.

M.505-1983
'BUTTERFLY' 1900
In the shape of a butterfly
Offset litho printed
Made by Barringer, Wallis & Manners for
Macfarlane, Lang & Co.
H.9cm. W.20cm. D.15cm.

M.506-1983
'TRUNK' 1900
A trunk
Offset litho printed with embossing
Made by Hudson Scott & Sons for Macfarlane
Lang & Co.
H.10cm. W.15.3cm. D.11.2cm.

M.507-1983
'STATIONERY CASE' 1901
Simulating wood with brass mounts; inner
liner opens to form a desk top
Offset litho printed
Made for Macfarlane, Lang & Co.
H.9.8cm. W.20.2cm. D.14cm.

M.508-1983
'STATIONERY CASE' 1901
Simulating wood with brass mounts, inner
liner opens to form a desk top
Offset litho printed
Made for Macfarlane, Lang & Co.
H.9.8cm. W.20.2cm. D.14cm.

M.509-1983
'ODDS AND ENDS' 1901
Offset litho printed with embossing
Made for Macfarlane, Lang & Co.
H.4.7cm. W.15.5cm. D.9.7cm.

M.510-1983
'PILLAR BOX' (Juvenile) 1901
A pillar-box money-box
Offset litho printed
Made for Macfarlane, Lang & Co.
H.11.7cm. Diam. 8cm.

M.511-1983
'STATIONERY CASE' 1902
With foldover lid
Offset litho printed, with embossing on lid
Made for Macfarlane, Lang & Co.
H.11cm. W.18.2cm. D.8.5cm.

M.512-1983
'MERMAID CASKET' 1902
A casket
Offset litho printed with embossing
Made for Macfarlane, Lang & Co.
H.8.5cm. W.20.2cm. D.12.9cm.

M.513-1983
'WEDGWOOD' 1902
An octagonal casket simulating Wedgwood
Jasperware, with handle and ceramic knob
Offset litho printed with embossing
Made for Macfarlane, Lang & Co.
H.13cm. Diam. 12.5cm.

M.514-1983
'VIOLIN CASE' 1903
A simulated wood violin case with handle
Offset litho printed
Made by Barringer, Wallis & Manners for
Macfarlane, Lang & Co.
H.7.5cm. W.24.3cm. D.9.2cm.

M.515-1983
'ANTIQUE COPPER' 1903
Offset litho printed simulating oxidised copper,
with embossing
Made by Barringer, Wallis & Manners for
Macfarlane, Lang & Co.
H.6.3cm. W.25.5cm. D.11cm.

M.516-1983
'MOTOR CAR' 1903
A motor car
Offset litho printed with embossing
Marked: Rd. 416498
Made by Hudson Scott & Sons for Macfarlane,
Lang & Co.
H.11.2cm. W.16.7cm. D.9.5cm.

M.517-1983
'WORCESTER CASKET' 1903
A casket on four ball feet
Offset litho printed with embossing
Made by Barringer, Wallis & Manners for
Macfarlane, Lang & Co.
H. 13.2cm. (excluding knob) W.18.3cm.
D.12.5cm.

M.518-1983
'FIRE ENGINE' 1904
A fire engine
Offset litho printed with embossing
Made by Hudson Scott & Sons for Macfarlane,
Lang & Co.
H.11.2cm. W.16.7cm. D.9.5cm.

M.519-1983
'CHIPPENDALE' 1904
A simulated wood chest with three opening
drawers
Offset litho printed
Made for Macfarlane, Lang & Co.
H.18cm. W.16.2cm. D.8.5cm.

M.520-1983
'ARCADIA' 1904
Simulating a bronze bas-relief set into a stained
oak wood box with rounded corners
Offset litho printed with embossing
Made for Macfarlane, Lang & Co.
H.5.2cm. W.22cm. D.14.4cm.

M.521-1983
'GEISHA' 1904
Offset litho printed
Made for Macfarlane, Lang & Co.
H.12cm. W.17.3cm. D.11.5cm.

M.522-1983
'CARNATION BISCUIT BOX' 1905
A handled jar with shaped sides
Offset litho printed
Made by Barringer, Wallis & Manners for
Macfarlane, Lang & Co.
H. 14cm. (excluding handle and knob)
W.14cm. D.14cm.

M.523-1983
'PRESERVE STAND' 1905
To be used as a holder for jam jars
Marked: Regd. No. 455742
Made by Barringer, Wallis & Manners for
Macfarlane, Lang & Co.
H. 16.5cm. (excluding handle) Diam. 14cm.

M.524-1983
'JUVENILE SATCHEL' 1906
A simulated straw satchel with foldover lid
Offset litho printed with embossing
Made for Macfarlane, Lang & Co.
H.10cm. W.12.2cm. D.6.1cm.

M.525-1983
Liner for Biscuit Tin: 'WORKBASKET' 1906
Offset litho printed
Made for Macfarlane, Lang & Co.
H.7.3cm. W.19cm. D.11.2cm.

M.526-1983
'DUTCH SCENES' (Juvenile) 1907
A jar with handle, on three ball feet
Offset litho printed
Made for Macfarlane, Lang & Co.
H. 11.5cm. (excluding handle and knob)
Diam. 9.5cm.

M.527-1983
'WHITE SWANS' 1907
A casket
Offset litho printed
Made by Barringer, Wallis & Manners for
Macfarlane, Lang & Co.
H.7.5cm. W.19cm. D.17cm.

M.528-1983
'LADY'S HANDBAG' (Juvenile) 1908
A handbag with metal chain handle
Offset litho printed with embossing
Made for Macfarlane, Lang & Co.
H.12.5cm. W.12cm. D.6.5cm.

M.529-1983
'REYNOLDS' 1908
A two-handled vase with reproductions of
J. Reynolds's paintings *Miss Bowles* and
The Age of Innocence
Offset litho printed
Made by Hudson Scott & Sons for Macfarlane,
Lang & Co.
H.18cm. (excluding knob) Diam.16cm.

M.530-1983
'STRAWBERRY BOX' 1909
A simulated woven straw punnet filled with
strawberries
Made by Barringer, Wallis & Manners for
Macfarlane, Lang & Co.
H.6cm. W.12.5cm. D.10.6cm.

M.531-1983
'WEDGWOOD' 1909
A two-handled vase
Offset litho printed
Made by Hudson & Scott & Sons for
Macfarlane, Lang & Co.
H.21cm. (excluding ceramic knob)
Diam.14cm

M.532-1983
'COACHING VASE' 1909
A two-handled vase on three ball feet
Offset litho printed
Made by Barringer, Wallis & Manners for
Macfarlane, Lang & Co.
H.14cm. Diam.18.5cm.

M.533-1983
'TAPESTRY HANDKERCHIEF BOX'
1909
Simulating tapestry
Offset litho printed
Made by Barringer, Wallis & Manners for
Macfarlane, Lang & Co.
H.6.2cm. W.17.6cm. D.16.8cm.

M.534-1983
'BIRD'S NEST' 1910
A bird's nest with eggs
Offset litho printed with embossing
Made by Barringer, Wallis & Manners for
Macfarlane, Lang & Co.
H.6.8cm. Diam.14cm.

M.535-1983
'MOZART CASKET' 1910
With a reproduction of a painting by August
Borckmann of Mozart and his sister playing
before the Empress Marie Theresa
Offset litho printed with embossing
Made by Barringer, Wallis & Manners for
Macfarlane, Lang & Co.
H.9.5cm. W.23.1cm. D.15cm.
(see advertising brochure)

M.536-1983
'HANDKERCHIEF BOX' 1910
Simulating tooled Russian leather; shaped
corners
Offset litho printed with embossing
Made by Barringer, Wallis & Manners for
Macfarlane, Lang & Co.
H.6.3cm. W.18.6cm. D.16.8cm.

M.537-1983
'YULE LOG' 1910
A log with an axe attached to the lid
Offset litho printed with embossing and
incising
Marked: Rd. 553615
Made for Macfarlane, Lang & Co.
H.13.3cm. (excluding axe) Diam.13.3cm.

M.538-1983
'CHINESE GLOVE BOX' 1911
Offset litho printed with embossing
Made by Barringer, Wallis & Manners for
Macfarlane, Lang & Co.
H.6.2cm. W.25.3cm. D.10.6cm.

M.539-1983
'MOTOR VAN' 1911
A wheeled toy in the form of Macfarlane, Lang
& Co's delivery van
Offset litho printed
Made by Hudson Scott & Sons for Macfarlane,
Lang & Co.
H.12cm. W.19.3cm. D.9cm.

M.540-1983
'ANVIL' 1911
An anvil, with a reproduction of E. Landseer's
painting Shoeing the Bay Mare on one side
Offset litho printed
Made by Hudson Scott & Sons for Macfarlane,
Lang & Co.
H.16cm. W.13cm. D.10cm.

M.541-1983
'WALL BOX' 1911
With two hooks for hanging on the wall
Offset litho printed simulating oxidized copper;
with embossing
Made by Barringer, Wallis & Manners for
Macfarlane, Lang & Co.
H.14cm. W.19.2cm. D.8.9cm.

M.542-1983
'TELEPHONE' 1911
A simulated wooden wall-mounted telephone
Offset litho printed with embossing
Made by Barringer, Wallis & Manners for
Macfarlane, Lang & Co.
H.22.2cm. W.9.5cm. D.8.5cm.

M.543-1983
'EBONY CASKET' 1912
Simulating ebony
Offset litho printed with embossing
Made by Barringer, Wallis & Manners for
Macfarlane, Lang & Co.
H.12cm. W.20.1cm. D.11.7cm.

M.544-1983
'TRUNK' 1913
A simulated leather luggage trunk
Offset litho printed with embossing
Made by Barringer, Wallis & Manners for
Macfarlane, Lang & Co.
H.6cm. W.14.2cm. D.9.2cm.

M.545-1983
'GOLF BAG' 1913
A golf bag with golf clubs
Offset litho printed with embossing
Made by Barringer, Wallis & Manners for
Macfarlane, Lang & Co.
H.27.5cm. Diam.8cm.

M.546-1983
'FLORAL' 1924
With shaped corners
Offset litho printed
Marked: No. 4058
Made for Macfarlane, Lang & Co.
H.5.9cm. W.18.6cm. D.16.8cm.

M.547-1983
'BLOSSOM' 1925
Offset litho printed
Marked: No. 4635
Made by Barringer, Wallis & Manners for
Macfarlane, Lang & Co.
H.6.5cm. W.25.7cm. D.11.2cm.

M.548-1983
'WALNUT' 1927
Offset litho printed
Made for Macfarlane, Lang & Co.
H.5.8cm. W.26.5cm. D.11.6cm.

M.549-1983
'WHITBY' 1928
Offset litho printed
Made by Barringer, Wallis & Manners for
Macfarlane, Lang & Co.
H.6.8cm. W.17.6cm. D.17.6cm.

M.550-1983
'YORK CAKE' 1929
Offset litho printed
Made for Macfarlane, Lang & Co.
H.8.1cm. W.19.3cm. D.14.2cm.

M.551-1983
'JAPANESE' 1929
With shaped corners
Offset litho printed
Made for Macfarlane, Lang & Co.
H.4.5cm. W.24.6cm. D.13.2cm.

M.552-1983
'ARABIAN' 1930
Offset litho printed
Made for Macfarlane, Lang & Co.
H.4.3cm. W.23.5cm. D.13cm.

M.553-1983
'BRIDGE BOX' 1930
Simulating wood
Offset litho printed
Made for Macfarlane, Lang & Co.
H.6cm. W.20.2cm. W.8.1cm.

M.554-1983
'HUNTING' 1930
Offset litho printed
Made for Macfarlane, Lang & Co.
H.7cm. W.17.6cm. D.17.6cm.

M.555-1983
'ROSE' 1931
Offset litho printed
Made for Macfarlane, Lang & Co.
H.6.4cm. W.26.5cm. D.11.6cm.

M.556-1983
'CRINOLINE' 1932
Offset litho printed
Made for Macfarlane, Lang & Co.
H.6.4cm. W.21.1cm. D.14.7cm.

M.557-1983
'ROSES' 1933
Offset litho printed
Made for Macfarlane, Lang & Co.
H.6.4cm. W.21.1cm. D.14.7cm.

M.558-1983
'ROBIN ADAIR' 1933
With a reproduction of Alexander Johnston's
painting Robin Adair on the lid; shaped corners
Offset litho printed
Made for Macfarlane, Lang & Co.
H.4.5cm. W.23.9cm. D.14.6cm.

M.559-1983
'GOLDEN GALLEON CASKET' 1934
Offset litho printed on imitation oxidised silver
plate
Designed by Webley
Made by Hudson Scott & Sons for Macfarlane,
Lang & Co.
H.8.7cm. W.25.6cm. D.19.4cm.

M.560-1983
'CLIPPER' 1934
Offset litho printed
Made for Macfarlane, Lang & Co.
H.4.3cm. W.21.3cm. D.15.7cm.

M.561-1983
'DAFFODIL' 1934
Octagonal
Offset litho printed
Made for Macfarlane, Lang & Co.
H.4cm. W.20cm.

M.562-1983
'TURNER CASKET' 1935
With a reproduction of J. M. W. Turner's
painting The Fighting Temeraire on the lid, and
of his Ulysses deriding Polyphemus on two sides
Offset litho printed
Made by Hudson Scott & Sons for Macfarlane
Lang & Co.
H.8.7cm. W.25.6cm. D.19.4cm.

M.563-1983
'REMBRANDT CASKET' 1936
With a reproduction of Rembrandt's painting
The Young Warrior (Man in Armour) on the lid
Offset litho printed
Made by Hudson Scott & Sons for Macfarlane,
Lang & Co.
H.8.7cm. W.25.6cm. D.19.4cm.

M.564-1983
'LONDON BRIDGE' 1936
With shaped ends
Offset litho printed
Made for Macfarlane, Lang & Co.
H.6cm. W.27.5cm. D.10.5cm.

M.565-1983
'COACHING DAYS' 1936
Oval
Offset litho printed
Made by Barringer, Wallis & Manners for
Macfarlane Lang & Co.
H.4cm. W.29cm. D.18.8cm.

M.566-1983
'DUTCH JAR' 1936
Offset litho printed
Made by Barringer, Wallis & Manners for
Macfarlane Lang & Co.
H.16cm. (excluding knob) Diam. 12.2cm.

M.567-1983
'NURSERY RHYMES' 1936
A house with an attached fence
Offset litho printed
Made for Macfarlane, Lang & Co.
H.12.5cm. W.16.5cm. D.11.3cm. (with fence
extended)

M.568-1983
'VILLAGE' 1936
Offset litho printed
Made for Macfarlane, Lang & Co.
H.7.1cm. W.23.6cm. D.13.1cm.

M.569-1983
'TYROLEAN CASKET' 1937
With a reproduction of J. MacWirter's painting
Meadows and Mountains on the lid
Offset litho printed
Made by Hudson Scott & Sons for Macfarlane,
Lang & Co.
H.8.7cm. W.25.6cm. D.19.4cm.

M.570-1983
'BISCUIT JAR' 1937
Offset litho printed
Made for Macfarlane, Lang & Co.
H.15cm. (excluding knob) Diam. 12.1cm.

M.571-1983
'CORONATION' 1937
With a portrait of King George VI and Queen
Elizabeth and Princess Elizabeth and Margaret
by Marcus Adams inset into the lid; shaped
corners
Offset litho printed with embossing
Made by Hudson Scott & Sons for Macfarlane,
Lang & Co.
H.5.6cm. W.23.7cm. D.19.7cm.

M.572-1983
'PAMELA' 1937
With a reproduction of Margaret Lindsay
Williams's painting Pamela on the lid
Offset litho printed
Made for Macfarlane, Lang & Co.
H.6.2cm. W.20.1cm. D.11.1cm.

M.573-1983
'MIDSHIPMAN' 1937
With a reproduction of G. Wilson Nesbit's
painting The Little Midshipman on the lid
Offset litho printed
Made for Macfarlane, Lang & Co.
H.4.4cm. W.20.5cm. D.16.6cm.

M.574-1983
'ENGINE' 1937
A model of L.N.E.R. express locomotive
'Silver Link', in its original cardboard box
Offset litho printed with embossing
Made for Macfarlane, Lang & Co.
H.6.5cm. W.34.5cm. D.6cm.

M.575-1983
'SILVER BOX' 1938
With a scene of shepherdesses in 18th Century
dress on the lid
Offset litho printed
Made by Barringer, Wallis & Manners for
Macfarlane, Lang & Co.
H.6.2cm. W.25.7cm. D.11.1cm.

M.576-1983
'TEA CADDY' 1938
Offset litho printed
Made for Macfarlane, Lang & Co.
H.17.2cm. W.10.2cm. D.10.2cm.

M.577-1983
'WONDERLAND COTTAGE' 1938
A money box in the form of a house decorated
with characters from *Alice in Wonderland* and
nursery rhymes
Offset litho printed
Made by Barringer, Wallis & Manners for
Macfarlane, Lang & Co.
H.13.6cm. W.15.7cm. D.6.2cm.

M.578-1983
'WATER-MILL' 1938
A toy water-mill, in its original cardboard box
Offset litho printed
Made for Macfarlane, Lang & Co.
H.18cm. W.12.2cm. D.8.3cm.

M.579-1983
'RED SCARF' 1938
With a reproduction of David S. Ewart's
painting *The Red Scarf* on the lid
Offset litho printed
Made for Macfarlane, Lang & Co.
H.4.8cm. W.20.6cm. D.13cm.

M.580-1983
'BUTTERFLY' 1939
Offset litho printed on gold textured ground
Made for Macfarlane, Lang & Co.
H.6.2cm. W.25.7cm. D.11.1cm.

M.581-1983
'BISCUIT JAR' 1939
Simulating an oriental ceramic jar with prunus
blossom decoration
Offset litho printed
Made for Macfarlane, Lang & Co.
H.17.5cm. (including knob)   Diam.10cm.

M.582-1983
'ROSES' 1939
Offset litho printed
Made for Macfarlane, Lang & Co.
H.7.1cm. W.17.5cm. D.17.5cm.

MACKENZIE & MACKENZIE

M.583-1983
'ALBANIA' c.1885
Transfer printed with embossing
Made for Mackenzie & Mackenzie
H.12cm. W.14cm. D.8.2cm.

M.584-1983
'A FAIRY TALE' c.1889
Transfer printed
Made for Mackenzie & Mackenzie
H.14.5cm. W.11cm. D.11cm.

M.585-1983
'PREPARING FOR THE CARNIVAL'
c.1890
With shaped ends
Transfer printed
Made for Mackenzie & Mackenzie
H.4.7cm. W.15.6cm. D.9.5cm.

M.586-1983
'LADIES RECREATIONS' c.1893
Triangular, with shaped sides
Offset litho printed
Made by Barringer, Wallis & Manners for
Mackenzie & Mackenzie
H.11.4cm. W.16.5cm. D.10.8cm.

M.587-1983
'RUSTIC' c.1890
With shaped sides
Offset litho printed
Made by Barringer, Wallis & Manners for
Mackenzie & Mackenzie
H.8.8cm. W.19cm. D.11cm.

M.588 and a-1983
URN c.1890
A pair of vases
Offset litho printed
Made for Mackenzie & Mackenzie
H.18cm. (excluding knob) W.14cm.

M.589-1983
PHOTO FRAME c.1904
With a photograph of Queen Mary when
Duchess of York inset in the lid (not issued
with the tin)
Offset litho printed with embossing
Manufacturer's mark: B. W. & M. Ltd.
Mansfield
Made by Barringer, Wallis & Manners for
Mackenzie & Mackenzie
H.4.7cm. W.21.3cm. D.17.2cm.

M.590-1983
DOLL'S HOUSE c.1908
A money box in the form of a house
Offset litho printed
Made by Barringer, Wallis & Manners for
Mackenzie & Mackenzie
H.11cm. W.10.4cm. D.7.5cm.

M.591-1983
PINCUSHION (Handkerchief Box) c.1909
Offset litho printed simulating inlaid wood,
with an inset velvet-covered pincushion
Manufacturer's mark: B. W. & M. Ltd.
Mansfield
Made by Barringer, Wallis & Manners for
Mackenzie & Mackenzie
H.6cm. (excluding pincushion) W.17.9cm.
D.15.9cm.

M.592-1983
PINCUSHION (Handkerchief Box) c.1909
Offset litho printed with embossing, and an
inset velvet-covered pincushion
Manufacturer's mark: B. W. & M. Ltd.
Mansfield
Made by Barringer, Wallis & Manners for
Mackenzie & Mackenzie
H.6cm. (excluding pincushion) W.17.9cm.
D.15.9cm.

M.593-1983
PINCUSHION (Glove box) c.1909
Offset litho printed with embossing, and an
inset velvet-covered pincushion
Manufacturer's mark: B. W. &. M. Ltd.
Mansfield
Made by Barringer, Wallis & Manners for
Mackenzie & Mackenzie
H.6cm (excluding pincushion) W.25.5cm.
D.11cm.

M.594-1983
CORONATION 1911
A two-handled urn with a portrait of Queen
Mary
Offset litho printed with embossing
Marked: Rd. 568115
Made by Hudson Scott & Sons for Mackenzie
& Mackenzie
H.22cm. W.12cm. D.11.5cm.

McVITIE & PRICE

M.595-1983
'QUEEN MARY' c.1891
Offset litho printed
Made for McVitie & Price
H.8.2cm. W.18.5cm. D.13.8cm.

M.596-1983
'RED RIDING HOOD' c.1891
Offset litho printed
Made for McVitie & Price
H.17.2cm. W.10cm. D.8cm.

M.597-1983
'AFRICAN HEROES' 1892
Offset litho printed
Made for McVitie & Price
H.12.5cm. W.12.6cm. D.9.3cm.

M.598-1983
'VICTORIA CROSS' 1893
With scenes depicting Army V.C. Heroes
Transfer printed with embossing
Manufacturer's mark: Hudson Scott Carlisle
Made by Hudson Scott & Sons for McVitie
& Price
H.13cm. W.14cm. D.8.4cm.

M.599-1983
'ACORN' 1893
Offset litho printed with embossing
Made for McVitie & Price
H.12.7cm. W.14cm. D.8.2cm.

M.600-1983
VICTORIA CROSS c.1894
With curved sides with scenes depicting
Navy V.C. heroes
Transfer printed with embossing
Made by Hudson Scott & Sons for McVitie
& Price
H.14cm. W.13.2cm. D.9.2cm.

M.601-1983
SUNFLOWER c.1895
Offset litho printed
Manufacturer's mark: Hudson Scott & Sons
Carlisle
Made by Hudson Scott & Sons for McVitie
& Price
H.13cm. W.14cm. D.8.3cm.

M.602-1983
'UNCLE TOM'S CABIN' 1896
Offset litho printed with embossing
Manufacturer's mark: Hudson Scott & Sons
Carlisle
Made by Hudson Scott & Sons for McVitie
& Price
H.16cm. W.12cm. D.8.2cm.

M.603-1983
SCOTTISH SONG c.1897
With shaped sides
Offset litho printed
Made for McVitie & Price
H.7.7cm. W.23cm. D.14.5cm.

M.604-1983
HIGHLAND STAGS c.1898
Offset litho printed
Made for McVitie & Price
H.8.2cm. W.24.3cm. D.10.5cm.

M.605-1983
'KITTENS' c.1899
Offset litho printed
Made for McVitie & Price
H.8.2cm. W.24.3cm. D.10.5cm.

M.606-1983
'ROLL TOP DESK' c.1901
A roll-top desk with simulated tambour lid
Offset litho printed with embossing
Made for McVitie & Price
H.14.3cm. W.17.3cm. D.14.2cm.

M.607-1983
BLOSSOMS CASKET c.1902
A casket on four ball feet
Offset litho printed with embossing
Made by Barringer, Wallis & Manners for
McVitie & Price
H.12cm. W.16.5cm. D.9.2cm.

M.608-1983
'HOLLY BOX' 1903
With curved sides
Offset litho printed with embossing
Made by Hudson Scott & Sons for McVitie
& Price
H.15.2cm. W.11.5cm. D.11.5cm.

M.609-1983
'HORSE SHOE' 1904
In the shape of a horse shoe
Offset litho printed with embossing
Made for McVitie & Price
H.9.5cm. W.15.2cm. D.14.5cm.

M.610-1983
'CAMEO' 1906
A casket
Offset litho printed
Made for McVitie & Price
H.7.4cm. W.19.4cm. D.11.4cm.

M.611-1983
'SUCRETTE' 1906
A kidney-shaped casket on feet, with handle
Offset litho printed imitating copper, with
embossing
Made by Barringer, Wallis & Manners for
McVitie & Price
H.15cm. W.17cm. D.7.7cm.

M.612-1983
'RAEBURN' 1909
Oval. The lid with a framed reproduction of
Raeburn's portrait of Mrs. Scott Moncrieff, with
a hook for displaying
Offset litho printed with embossing
Made by Barringer, Wallis & Manners for
McVitie & Price
H.6cm.   W.20.6cm.   D.16cm.

M.613-1983
'LOUVRE' 1909
The lid with a framed reproduction after
Mme Vigée-Le Brun's self-portrait with her
child, with a hook for displaying
Offset litho printed with embossing
Manufacturer's mark: Hudson Scott & Sons
Ltd. Carlisle, England. Rd. 547, 632
Made by Hudson Scott & Sons for McVitie
& Price
H.6.5cm.   W.17.5cm.   D.14.6cm.

M.614-1983
'MATERNAL LOVE' 1910
With shaped ends and reproductions of
Romney's painting A Lady with a child and
Reynolds's Mrs. Hoare and her son
Offset litho printed with embossing
Manufacturer's mark: Hudson Scott & Sons
Ltd. Carlisle
Made by Hudson Scott and Sons for McVitie
& Price
H.17cm.   W.20cm.   D.7.7cm.

M.615-1983
'DELIA' 1910
With a reproduction of G. Morland's painting
Delia in the Garden on the lid; with a hook for
displaying
Offset litho printed with embossing
Made by Barringer, Wallis & Manners for
McVitie & Price
H.5.7cm.   W.21.6cm.   D.17.5cm.

M.616-1983
'BLUEBIRD' 1911
A bird
Offset litho printed with embossing
Made by Barringer, Wallis & Manners for
McVitie & Price
H.23.5cm.

M.617-1983
'No. 10 DOWNING STREET' 1924
This tin was never issued
Offset litho printed
Made for McVitie & Price
H.7cm.   W.18.3cm.   D.12.5cm.

M.618-1983
'LORRAINE' 1932
With a reproduction of Lancret's painting
A Cup of Chocolate on the lid; curved ends
Offset litho printed
Made by Barringer, Wallis & Manners for
McVitie & Price
H.3.8cm.   W.23.5cm.   D.15.2cm.

M.619-1983
'BLUE TIN' 1933
With a reproduction of James Ward's painting
The Mouse's Petition on the lid
Offset litho printed
Marked: No. 16409
Made by Barringer, Wallis & Manners for
McVitie & Price
H.6.8cm.   W.18.3cm.   D.10cm.

M.620-1983
'CARNIVAL' 1933
With a reproduction of George Moorland's
painting Children playing at Soldiers on the lid;
curved ends
Offset litho printed
Made by Barringer, Wallis & Manners for
McVitie & Price
H.3.8cm.   W.23.5cm.   D.15.2cm.

M.621-1983
'CABINETTE' 1933
A three-drawer cabinet on legs
Offset litho printed with embossing
Made by Barringer, Wallis & Manners for
McVitie & Price
H15.5cm.   W.21cm.   D.13cm.

M.622-1983
'DOVEDALE' 1935
With a coaching scene on the lid; shaped
corners
Offset litho printed
Made by Barringer Wallis & Manners for
McVitie & Price
H.5.2cm.   W.25.5cm.   D.16.6cm.

M.623-1983
'MIRANDA' 1935
With a reproduction of W. Hamilton's painting
Feeding Children on the lid
Offset litho printed
Made by Barringer, Wallis & Manners for
McVitie & Price
H.6.8cm.   W.18.3cm.   D.10cm.

M.624-1983
'SILVER BLUE' 1935
With shaped corners
Offset litho printed
Made by Barringer, Wallis & Manners for
McVitie & Price
H.7.3cm.   W.27.3cm.   D.10.5cm.

M.625-1983
'DEVON' 1935
Offset litho printed
Made for McVitie & Price
H.8.5cm.   Diam.18cm.

M.626-1983
SILVER JUBILEE 1935
With portraits of George V and Queen Mary
on the lid
Offset litho printed
Made for McVitie & Price
H.4.4cm.   W.13.8cm.   D.11cm.

M.627-1983
'RUBY' 1936
With a reproduction of a painting of a cottage
interior on the lid
Offset litho printed
Made by Barringer, Wallis & Manners for
McVitie & Price
H.6.8cm.   W.18.3cm.   D.10cm.

M.628-1983
'BLUE TIN' 1937
With a reproduction of a landscape painting on
the lid
Offset litho printed
Made by Barringer, Wallis & Manners for
McVitie & Price
H.6.8cm.   W.18.3cm.   D.10cm.

M.629-1983
'CHOCOLATE TABLE' 1937
With a reproduction of Mme Doré's painting
A Girl Holding a Rose on the lid
Offset litho printed with embossing
Made for McVitie & Price
H.6.7cm.   Diam.12.2cm.

M.630-1983
'FLORAL' 1937
Offset litho printed with embossing
Made for McVitie & Price
H.6cm.   W.14cm.   D.14cm.

M.631-1983
'KIDDIES' 1938
With reproductions of Randolph Caldecott's
1880 illustrations to Sing a Song of Sixpence;
shaped corners
Offset litho printed
Made by Huntley, Boorne & Stevens for
McVitie & Price
H.14cm.   W.10.5cm.   D.10.5cm.

M.632-1983
'WESTMINSTER' 1938
With a view of the Palace of Westminster on
the lid; shaped corners
Offset litho printed with embossing
Made for McVitie & Price
H.5.5cm.   W.26cm.   D.11.2cm.

M.633-1983
'STORK' 1938
Offset litho printed with embossing
Made for McVitie & Price
H.11.5cm.   Diam.12.2cm.

M.634-1983
'ROSE' 1938
Offset litho printed with embossing
Made for McVitie & Price
H.4.5cm.   Diam.20.2cm.

M.635-1983
'CARNIVAL' 1938
With a reproduction of a painting of children
playing on the lid
Offset litho printed
Made by Barringer, Wallis & Manners for
McVitie & Price
H.6.8cm.   W.18.3cm.   D.10cm.

M.636-1983
'PETER RABBIT' 1939
With illustrations after Beatrix Potter's Tales
of Peter Rabbit; shaped corners
Offset litho printed
Made by Huntley, Boorne & Stevens for
McVitie & Price
H.14cm.   W.10.5cm.   D.10.5cm.

M.637-1983
'CAMEO' 1939
Offset litho printed with embossing
Made for McVitie & Price
H.6cm.   W.15.9cm.   D.17.2cm.

M.638-1983
'JERSEY' 1939
Simulating embroidery
Offset litho printed
Made for McVitie & Price
H.5.5cm.   W.24.3cm.   D.9.7cm.

M.639-1983
'CHELSEA' 1939
With a view of Chelsea Walk, Chelsea. c.1840
on the lid; shaped front edge
Offset litho printed
Made for McVitie & Price
H.5.3cm.   W.24.3cm.   D.9.9cm.

PEEK FREAN & CO.

M.640-1983
'TAMBOUR' (beige) c.1881
Transfer printed
Made by Peek Frean & Co.
H.17.7cm.   Diam. 13.3cm.
(see brochure in Prints & Drawings)

M.641-1983
'TAMBOUR' (green) c.1881
Transfer printed
Made for Peek Frean & Co.
H.17.7cm.   Diam. 13.3cm.
(see brochure in Prints & Drawings)

M.642-1983
NATIONS c.1882
Transfer printed
Made for Peek Frean & Co.
H.6cm.   Diam. 14.8cm.

M.643-1983
JOHN GILPIN c.1884
Transfer printed
Made for Peek Frean & Co.
H.9cm.   W.16.5cm.   D.11.4cm.

M.644-1983
'CHASE' 1887
Offset litho printed
Made for Peek Frean & Co.
H.4.5cm.   W.15.5cm.   D.9.8cm.

M.645-1983
CHILDREN 1888
Offset litho printed
Made for Peek Frean & Co.
H.4.5cm.   W.15.5cm.   D.9.8cm.

M.646-1983
'TOURNAMENT' 1888
Fitted with a lock
Offset litho printed
Made for Peek Frean & Co.
H4.5cm.   W.15.5cm.   D.9.8cm.

M.647-1983
'FISHERGIRL' 1889
Offset litho printed
Made for Peek Frean & Co.
H.7.5cm.   W.16.5cm.   D.10.4cm.

M.648-1983
HUNTSMEN c.1890
Offset litho printed
Made for Peek Frean & Co. (for export)
H.5.8cm.   W.15.4cm.   D.8.8cm.

M.649-1983
'BEANSTALK' 1892
Offset litho printed
Made for Peek Frean & Co.
H.4.5cm. W.15.5cm. D.9.8cm.

M.650-1983
'LANDSEER' 1893
With reproductions of Landseer's paintings
Dignity and Impudence; *Peace*; *War*; *Hunted
Stag*; *Friends at the Trough*
Offset litho printed
Made for Peek Frean & Co.
H.17.5cm. Diam. 13.5cm.

M.651-1983
'ARAB' 1893
With shaped corners
Offset litho printed
Made for Peek Frean & Co.
H.12.2cm. W.12cm. D.12cm.

M.652-1983
DAIRYMAID c.1893
Offset litho printed
Made for Peek Frean & Co. (for export)
H.7cm. W.17.6cm. D.12.2cm.

M.653-1983
'CASTILIAN' 1894
Offset litho printed
Made for Peek Frean & Co.
H.4.5cm. W.15.5cm. D.9.8cm.

M.654-1983
'GOBLIN' 1895
Semicircular, with shaped sides
Offset litho printed
Made for Peek Frean & Co.
H.7.7cm. W.26.2cm. D.14.3cm.

M.655-1983
'ROYAL' 1896
With shaped sides
Offset litho printed
Made for Peek Frean & Co.
H.7cm. W.19cm. D.17cm.

M.656-1983
'FUR TRADERS' 1896
With shaped corners
Offset litho printed
Made for Peek Frean & Co.
H.6cm. W.17cm. D.11.7cm.

M.657-1983
'SEASONS' 1897
Offset litho printed
Made for Peek Frean & Co.
H.11.5cm. W.7.9cm. D.7.9cm.

M.658-1983
'DIAMOND JUBILEE' 1897
Offset litho printed with embossing
Made for Peek Frean & Co.
H.13cm. W.14cm. D.8.5cm.
(see brochure)

M.659-1983
'MOSAIC' 1898
With clasp fastening
Offset litho printed
Made for Peek Frean & Co.
H.5.8cm. W.17.3cm. D.15cm.

M.660-1983
'VERSAILLES' 1899
With shaped sides
Offset litho printed
Made for Peek Frean & Co.
H.13.3cm. W.14.5cm. D.11.8cm.

M.661-1983
'ANEMONE' 1899
With clasp fastening
Offset litho printed
Made for Peek Frean & Co.
H.5.8cm. W.17.3cm. D.15cm.

M.662-1983
'SATCHEL' 1899
A simulated crocodile skin handbag with
collapsible handle
Offset litho printed with embossing
Made for Peek Frean & Co.
H. (excluding handle) 12.7cm. W.21.5cm.
D.5.3cm.

M.663-1983
'HORSESHOE' 1900
In the shape of a horseshoe
Offset litho printed with embossing
Made for Peek Frean & Co.
H.4.5cm. W.16.2cm. D.14.2cm.

M.664 and a-1983
'VASE' 1900
A pair of vases; the lids made to be used as the
bases
Offset litho printed with embossing
Marked: Regd. No. 36959b
Made for Peek Frean & Co.
H.18.5cm. Diam. 10cm.

M.665-1983
'DERBY' 1902
Shaped oval
Offset litho printed
Marked: No. 7079
Made by Barringer, Wallis & Manners for
Peek Frean & Co.
H.12cm. W.15.5cm. D.11.7cm.

M.666-1983
'SANDWICH BOX' 1903
A satchel with collapsible handle
Offset litho printed
Made for Peek Frean & Co.
H.12cm. (excluding handle) W.13.1cm.
D.5.3cm.

M.667-1983
'SILVER' 1904
Imitation oxidised silver with embossing, with
an offset litho printed central panel of girls
Marked: Patent No. 18593
Made by Hudson Scott & Sons for Peek Frean
& Co.
H.5.4cm. W.19.6cm. D.7.3cm.

M.668-1983
'COFFER' 1905
A casket on feet
Offset litho printed
Made by Barringer, Wallis & Manners for
Peek Frean & Co.
H.10.7cm. W.18.2cm. D.12cm.

M.669-1983
'CASKET' 1905
A casket; with a picture of a dog on the lid
Offset litho printed
Made by Barringer, Wallis & Manners for
Peek Frean & Co.
H.7.5cm. W.17cm. D.18.8cm.

M.670-1983
'PRIMROSE' 1906
Offset litho printed
Made for Peek Frean & Co.
H.4.3cm. W.12.5cm. D.12.5cm.

M.671-1983
'PEACOCK' 1906
A casket on ball feet
Offset litho printed simulating inlaid mosaic
work
Made for Peek Frean & Co.
H.9cm. W.25cm. D.13.2cm.

M.672-1983
'VINEYARD' 1906
Offset litho printed with embossing
Made for Peek Frean & Co.
H.6.5cm. W.25.4cm. D.11cm.

M.673-1983
'DOMINO' 1906
Offset litho printed
Made for Peek Frean & Co.
H.3.4cm. W.23.2cm. D.8.2cm.

M.674-1983
'CABIN TRUNK' c.1913
A simulated leather suitcase
Offset litho printed with embossing
Made by Hudson Scott & Sons for Peek Frean
& Co.
H.6cm. W.15cm. D.9cm.

M.675-1983
'SHIP' c.1913
Offset litho printed
Made for Peek Frean & Co.
H.5.8cm. W.15.4cm. D.8.8cm.

M.676 (a)-(e)-1983
'CASTLE' 1923
A tower with sectioned wall extensions
(a) -with 4 wall sections: 2 flags inside
(b) - with 3 wall sections
(c) - with 3 wall sections
(d) - with 2 wall sections
(e) - with 3 wall sections
Offset litho printed
Each with manufacturer's mark: H. B. & S. Ltd
Reading
Made by Huntley, Boorne & Stevens for
Peek Frean & Co.
Tower: H.16.8cm. W.6.5cm. D.6.5cm.
Wall sections: H.11.5cm. W.6 or 7cm.

M.677-1983
'TULIP' 1929
Oval
Offset litho printed
Made for Peek Frean & Co.
H.3.5cm. W.25.7cm. D.14.7cm.

M.678-1983
'KASHMIR' 1930
Offset litho printed
Made for Peek Frean & Co.
H.3.3cm. W.22.5cm. D.11.7cm.

M.679-1983
'COCOANUT SHIES' 1931
Containing backboard: stand with 5 wooden
coconuts: and stand for shooting the wooden
ball
Offset litho printed base; the lid and sides with
printed paper labels
Made for Peek Frean & Co.
H.5.5cm. W.21.8cm. D.14cm

M.680-1983
'BURNE JONES' 1932
With a reproduction of Burne-Jones' painting
King Cophetua and the Beggermaid on the lid;
with shaped corners
Offset litho printed
Made by Barringer, Wallis & Manners for
Peek Frean & Co.
H.6.3cm. W.22.3cm. D.15.3cm.

M.681-1983
'WELLS MARKET' 1933
With shaped corners
Offset litho printed
Made by Barringer, Wallis & Manners for
Peek Frean & Co.
H.3.8cm. W.18.6cm. D.16.8cm.

M.682-1983
'SEA ROVERS' 1933
With shaped corners
Offset litho printed
Made for Peek Frean & Co.
H.6cm. W.23.2cm. D.15.3cm.

M.683-1983
CHRYSANTHEMUMS c.1933
Offset litho printed
Made for Peek Frean & Co. (for export)
H.5.8cm. W.15.4cm. D.8.8cm.

M.684-1983
SATCHEL c.1933
Imitation snakeskin satchel with collapsible
handle
Offset litho printed
Made for Peek Frean & Co.
H.5.5cm. W.20.5cm. D.12.8cm.

M.685-1983
'COACHING DAYS' 1934
With shaped corners
Offset litho printed
Made by Barringer, Wallis & Manners for
Peek Frean & Co.
H.3.8cm. W.16.8cm. D.18.6cm.

M.686-1983
'GRANDFATHER CLOCK' 1935
A grandfather clock with scenes from *Hickory
Dickory Dock*
Offset litho printed
Made by Hudson Scott & Sons for Peek Frean
& Co.
H.17cm. W.6.9cm. D.6.9cm.

M.687-1983
'HAPPY REFLECTIONS' 1935
With a reproduction of Mme Y. G. Ledret's
painting *Happy Reflections* on the lid; shaped
corners
Offset litho printed
Made by Barringer, Wallis & Manners for
Peek Frean & Co.
H.5.7cm.   W.25.7cm.   D.16.6cm.

M.688-1983
'LOCH MAREE' c.1935
With a reproduction of Sutton Palmer's
painting *Loch Maree* on the lid
Offset litho printed
Made for Peek Frean & Cc.
H.4.5cm.   W.24.5cm.   D.18.5cm.

M.689-1983
'CLOVELLY' 1936
Offset litho printed
Manufacturer's mark: H. B. & S. Ltd. R.
Made by Huntley, Boorne & Stevens for
Peek Frean & Co.
H.3.8cm.   W.21.7cm.   D.14.5cm.

M.690-1983
'LOCH GARRY' 1936
With a reproduction of Alfred de Bréanski's
painting *Loch Garry* on the lid
Offset litho printed
Made for Peek Frean & Co.
H.4.5cm.   W.24.5cm.   D.18.5cm.

M.691-1983
CORONATION ED. VIII 1937
With a portrait of Edward VIII on the lid;
shaped front side
Offset litho printed
Made by Hudson Scott & Sons for Peek Frean
& Co.
H.6.7cm.   W.16cm.   D.12cm.

M.692-1983
CORONATION 1937
With portraits of George VI and Queen
Elizabeth after photographs by Speaight Ltd. on
the lid; shaped front side
Offset litho printed
Made by Hudson Scott & Sons for Peek Frean
& Co.
H.6.7cm.   W.16cm.   D.12cm.

M.693-1983
'BOUDOIR' 1937
One shaped side
Offset litho printed
Made for Peek Frean & Co.
H.5cm.   W.16cm.   D.15.3cm.

M.694-1983
'WORK BOX' 1939
Simulating pokerwork
Offset litho printed with incised decoration
Made by Barringer, Wallis & Manners for
Peek Frean & Co.
H.8.5cm.   W.16.7cm.   D.11.2cm.

OTHER COMPANIES

M.695-1983
PILLAR BOX c.1897
A pillar box for use as a money-box
Offset litho printed
Manufacturer's mark: B.W.M. Ltd. Mansfield
Made by Barringer, Wallis & Manners for
A1 Biscuit Company
H.15.5cm.   Diam. 8cm.

M.696-1983
STRAW BASKET c.1898
A simulated straw basket, with folding handle
(catch missing)
Offset litho printed
Manufacturer's mark: B. W. & M. Ltd.
Mansfield
Made by Barringer, Wallis & Manners for
A1 Biscuit Company
H.7 cm. (excluding handle)   W.15.6cm.
D.8cm.

M.697-1983
OAK BARREL c.1899
A simulated oak barrel with handle
Offset litho printed
Made for A1 Biscuit Company
H.10.5cm. (excluding handle)   Diam. 8.5cm.

M.698-1983
SILVER JUBILEE 1935
With portraits of George V and Queen Mary on
the lid and views of royal palaces
Offset litho printed
Made for Bee Bee Biscuits
H.9.2cm.   W.24.8cm.   D.9cm.

M.699-1983
ACTRESSES c.1891
Offset litho printed
Made for Thomas Charnley
H.14.5cm.   W.10cm.   D.10cm.

M.700-1983
KINGFISHER c.1895
Offset litho printed
Manufacturer's mark: H. Scott & Sons
Carlisle
Made by Hudson Scott & Sons for Thomas
Charnley
H.14.5cm.   W.10cm.   D.10cm.

M.701-1983
'COUNTRY COTTAGE' 1935
Offset litho printed
Manufacturer's mark: H. B. & S. Ltd. Reading
Made by Huntley, Boorne & Stevens for
Chiltonian Ltd.
H.3.9cm.   W.21.5cm.   D.16cm.

M.702-1983
'CORNFLOWER' 1938
Offset litho printed
Made by Barringer, Wallis & Manners for
Chiltonian Ltd.
H.6.2cm.   W.25.8cm.   D.11.1cm.

M.703-1983
'NURSERY RHYMES' 1938
With scenes from *Little Bo-Peep*; *Little Boy
Blue*; *Mary, Mary, quite contrary*; *Tom, Tom,
the Piper's Son* and *Humpty Dumpty*; shaped
corners
Offset litho printed
Made for Chiltonian Ltd.
H.14cm.   W.11cm.   D.11cm.

M.704-1983
SHAKESPEARE c.1893
Hexagonal
Offset litho printed
Made for W. Dunmore & Son
H.15cm.   W.13.8cm.   D.8.3cm.

M.705-1983
LIGHTHOUSE c.1894
For use as a money-box
Offset litho printed
Manufacturer's mark: Barclay & Fry
Made by Barclay & Fry for W. Dunmore & Son
H.18cm.   Diam. 9.1cm.

M.706-1983
PILLAR BOX c.1897
A pillar box, for use as a money-box
Offset litho printed
Manufacturer's mark: B. W. & M. Ltd.
Mansfield
Made by Barringer, Wallis & Manners for
W. Dunmore & Son
H.15.5cm.   Diam. 8cm.

M.707-1983
BASKET c.1898
A simulated straw basket with folding handle
and clasp
Offset litho printed
Manufacturer's mark: B. W. & M. Ltd.
Mansfield
Made by Barringer, Wallis & Manners for
W. Dunmore & Son
H.7cm. (excluding handle)   W.15.6cm.
D.8cm.

M.708-1983
CRESCENT BASKET c.1898
Semicircular basket, with folding handle and
clasp
Offset litho printed
Manufacturer's mark: Printed by B. W. & M.
Ltd. Mansfield
Made by Barringer, Wallis & Manners for
W. Dunmore & Son
H.8.5cm.   W.14.5cm.   D.9.2cm.

M.709-1983
OAK BARREL c.1899
A simulated oak barrel with handle
Offset litho printed
Made for W. Dunmore & Son
H.10.5cm. (excluding handle)   Diam. 8.5cm.

M.710-1983
PINCUSHION c.1909
With a pincushion on the lid
Offset litho printed with embossing
Made by Burnett Ltd. for W. Dunmore & Son.
H.6.2cm. (excluding pincushion)   W.25.5cm.
D.11cm.

M.711-1983
MONEY BOX c.1910
A chest with handle
Offset litho printed with embossing
Marked: No. 11656
Made for W. Dunmore & Son
H.5.5cm.   W.14cm.   D.8.4cm.

M.712-1983
PANSY VASE c.1910
A vase
Offset litho printed with embossing
Marked: No. 10825
Made by Barringer, Wallis & Manners for
W. Dunmore & Son
H.16.5cm.   W.13cm.   D.12.7cm.

M.713-1983
'GLOAMING' c.1912
A two-handled vase
Offset litho printed
Made by Hudson Scott & Son for W. Dunmore
& Son
H.16.7cm.   W.6.8cm.   D.6.8cm.

M.714-1983
DARTBOARD c.1928
The lid in the form of a dartboard with a hook
for hanging
Offset litho printed
Marked: No. 4706
Made by Barringer, Wallis & Manners for
W. Dunmore & Son
H.4.2cm.   W.20.2cm.   D.20.2cm.

M.715-1983
'TRUNK' c.1903
A trunk
Offset litho printed with embossing
Marked: Registered
Made by Hudson Scott & Sons for Far Famed
Cake Co.
H.9cm.   W.12.3cm.   D.8.2cm.

M.716-1983
GREENHOUSE c.1905
A greenhouse
Offset litho printed
Made by Barringer, Wallis & Manners for
Far Famed Cake Co.
H.8.7cm.   W.14.3cm.   D.7.8cm.

M.717-1983
ROYAL MARRIAGE c.1889
Issued in commemoration of the marriage of
Princess Louise of Wales (eldest daughter of
Albert Edward, Prince of Wales) and
Alexander Duff, Earl of Fife, whose portraits
appear on the lid. Also scenes of their residences,
Duff House, Banff; Sheen Lodge; Mar Lodge,
Braemar
Transfer-printed
Made for Graham Bros.
H.7.7cm.   W.18cm.   D.11.5cm.

M.718-1983
ARAB c.1890
With shaped corners
Offset litho printed
Made for S. Henderson & Sons
H.4.7cm.   W.15.6cm.   D.9.5cm.

M.719-1893
'MILK CAN' 1900
A simulated wooden milk churn
Offset litho printed with embossing
Made for S. Henderson & Sons
H.18.3cm.   Diam. 12.6cm.

M.720-1983
APPLE BLOSSOM c.1902
Offset litho printed
Marked: Rd. 419702
Made for S. Henderson & Sons
H.7.5cm.   W.14.3cm.   D.7.6cm.

M.721-1983
ART NOUVEAU CASKET c.1905
A casket on feet
Offset litho printed
Made by Barringer, Wallis & Manners for
S. Henderson & Sons
H.10.7cm.   W.18.2cm.   D.12cm.

58

M.722-1983
DUTCH c.1908
Offset litho printed
Made by Hudson Scott & Sons for S. Henderson
& Sons
H.5.6cm.   W.12.8cm.   D.12.8cm.

M.723-1983
BOOKSTAND c.1910
Five books in a stand
Offset litho printed
Manufacturer's mark: Hudson Scott & Sons
Ltd. Carlisle
Made by Hudson Scott & Sons for S. Henderson
& Sons
H.11cm.   W.11.7cm.   D8.1cm.

M.724-1983
'LOG CABIN' c.1911
A log cabin
Offset litho printed with embossing
Marked: Rd 575667
Made by Hudson Scott & Sons for S. Henderson
& Sons
H.12cm.   W.16.7cm.   D.12.5cm.

M.725-1983
'FLORAL' c.1912
With shaped corners
Offset litho printed with embossing
Made for S. Henderson & Sons
H.3.8cm.   W.23.3cm.   D.15.3cm.

M.726-1983
PEACOCK CHEST c.1889
With curved front edge
Offset litho printed
Manufacturer's mark: Hudson Scott & Sons,
Carlisle
Made by Hudson Scott & Sons for George
Herbert
H.8.3cm.   W.16cm.   D.12cm.

M.727-1983
CHICKENS c.1905
With curved sides
Offset litho printed, with wool handles
Made for George Herbert Ltd.
H.8cm.   W.12.3cm.   D.9.5cm.

M.728-1983
THE HUNT c.1907
Offset litho printed
Manufacturer's mark: Hudson Scott & Sons,
Carlisle
Made by Hudson Scott & Sons for George
Herbert Ltd.
H.6.5cm.   W.14cm.   D.8.4cm.

M.729-1983
'SENTRY BOX' c.1900
Offset litho printed with embossed figures of
soldiers
Made for John Hill & Son
H.16.5cm.   W.6.8cm.   D.6.8cm.

M.730-1983
'PUPPY' 1903
Offset litho printed
Marked: Rd. 404403
Made for John Hill & Son
H.5.5cm.   W.10cm.   D.7.8cm

M.731-1983
THISTLE POT c.1926
Aluminium, embossed
Manufacturer's mark: N. C. J. Ltd.
Made by N. C. Joseph Ltd. for Hughes
H.12.5cm.   W.16.5cm.

M.732-1983
WHEEL OF FORTUNE c.1934
Octagonal
Offset litho printed
Made for Hughes
H.9cm.   W.11.5cm.   D.11.5cm.

M.733-1983
'HANDBAG' c.1912
A simulated snakeskin handbag with wool
handles, and clasp
Offset litho printed with embossing
Made for George Kemp
H.5cm.   W.14.7cm.   D.11.8cm.

M.734-1983
SILVER JUBILEE 1935
A pillar box to be used as a money box, with
portraits of George V and Queen Mary
Offset litho printed
Made for Andrew G. Kidd Ltd.
H.11cm.   Diam.5.4cm

M.735-1983
SATCHEL c.1903
A satchel with folding handle
Offset litho printed with embossing
Made for Marsh & Co.
H.12cm. (excluding handle)   W.12.8cm.
D.5.2cm.

M.736-1983
KING OF HEARTS c.1898
With handle
Offset litho printed
Made for McCall & Stephen
H.4cm.   W.20.5cm.   D.15.3cm.

M.737-1983
ART NOUVEAU BARREL c.1905
With handle
Offset litho printed
Manufacturer's mark: B. W. & M. Ltd.
Mansfield
Made by Barringer, Wallis & Manners for
Meredith & Drew Ltd.
H.13cm. (excluding handle & knob)
Diam.14cm.

M.738-1983
CARVED IVORY HANDKERCHIEF BOX
c.1911
A casket
Offset litho printed with embossing
Manufacturer's mark: Regd. No. 582129
B.W. & M. Ltd., Mansfield
Made by Barringer, Wallis & Manners for
Meredith & Drew Ltd.
H.6.5cm.   W.21cm.   D.19cm.

M.739-1983
PARISIEN HANDKERCHIEF BOX
c.1911
With shaped corners
Offset litho printed with embossing
Made by Barringer, Wallis & Manners for
Meredith & Drew Ltd.
H.6cm.   W.19.7cm.   D.17.1cm.

M.740-1983
ROMEO AND JULIET c.1928
Offset litho printed
Made by Barringer, Wallis & Manners for
Meredith & Drew Ltd.
H.6cm.   W.21.7cm.   D.17.6cm.

M.741-1983
CHEESE SANDWICH INN c.1934
An inn
Offset litho printed
Manufacturer's mark: H.B. & S. Ltd., Reading
Made by Huntley, Boorne & Stevens for
Meredith & Drew Ltd.
H.12.5cm.   W.15.6cm.   D.10cm.

M.742-1983
DRAGON-FLY c.1911
A casket
Imitation oxidized copper finish, with
embossing
Made by Barringer, Wallis & Manners for
R. Middlemass & Son Ltd.
H.6.5cm.   W.21cm.   D.19cm.

M.743-1983
WORK BASKET c.1898
A basket with simulated quilted lid, and handle
Offset litho printed
Made for Palmer Bros.
H.6cm.   W.14.3cm.   D.10.5cm.

M.744-1983
SMALL HAMPER c.1900
A simulated wicker hamper with handle
Offset litho printed with embossing
Made by Hudson Scott & Sons for Palmer
Bros.
H.7.3cm.   W.14.3cm.   D.7.8cm.

M.745-1983
'TRUNK' c.1903
A trunk
Offset litho printed with embossing
Made by Hudson Scott & Sons for Palmers Bros.
H.9cm.   W.12.3cm.   D.8.2cm.

M.746-1983
H.R.H. PRINCESS VICTORIA AT
TUNBRIDGE WELLS IN 1822 c.1934
Offset litho printed
Designed by Edward Bawden (b. 1903)
Made for A. Romany & Co. Ltd.
H.5.6cm.   W.21.7cm.   D.14cm.

M.747-1983
CAVALIER c.1898
With curved sides
Offset litho printed
Made for Spillers Nephews Biscuit Co.
H.12cm.   W.15.8cm.   D.12.2cm.

M.748-1983
PARROT CAGE c.1896
Offset litho printed
Made for John Walker Ltd.
H.12.5cm. (excluding handle)   Diam. 9.2cm.

M.749-1983
DEVONSHIRE c.1912
With a portrait of the Duchess of Devonshire on
the lid
Offset litho printed
Made by Hudson Scott & Sons for John
Whittaker & Sons
H.6cm.   W.14cm.   D.14cm.

M.750-1983
COLOURED DRAGON-FLY c.1912
A casket
Offset litho printed with embossing
Made by Barringer, Wallis & Manners for
L. Wright & Sons
H.6.5cm.   W.21cm.   D.19cm.